THE LAW OF SPECIAL EDUCATIONAL NEEDS
A Guide to the Education Act 1981

THE LAW OF SPECIAL EDUCATIONAL NEEDS

A Guide to the Education Act 1981

BRYAN COX, LL.B,
of the Middle Temple and the North-eastern Circuit, Barrister.

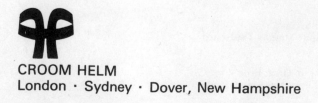

CROOM HELM
London · Sydney · Dover, New Hampshire

© 1985 Bryan Cox
Croom Helm Ltd, Provident House, Burrell Row,
Beckenham, Kent BR3 1AT
Croom Helm Australia Pty Ltd, Suite 4, 6th Floor,
64–76 Kippax Street, Surry Hills, NSW 2010, Australia
New in paperback 1985

British Library Cataloguing in Publication Data

Cox, Brian, 19 - - - -
    The law of special educational needs.
    1. Great Britain. Education Act 1981
    2. Educational law and legislation—England
    3. Exceptional children—Education—Law and
    legislation—England
    I. Title
    344.204′791   KD3605

    ISBN 0-7099-3429-7
    ISBN 0-7099-3498-x (Pbk)

Croom Helm, 51 Washington Street, Dover,
New Hampshire 03820, USA

Library of Congress Cataloging in Publication Data

Cox, Bryan, 1955–
    The law of special educational needs.

    Includes index.
    1. Handicapped children—Education—Law and
    legislation—Great Britain.
    I. Title.
    KD3664.C68 1984   371.9   84-15600
    ISBN 0-7099-3429-7
    ISBN 0-7099-3498-x (Pbk)

Photoset in English Times
by Patrick and Anne Murphy Typesetters,
Highcliffe, Dorset.

Printed and bound in Great Britain by
Biddles Ltd, Guildford and King's Lynn

CONTENTS

Contents

ABBREVIATIONS

'The Act'	The Education Act 1981
'Principal Act'	The Education Act 1944
'Statemented Child'	A child in respect of whom a local education authority has made a statement under Section 7 of the Education Act 1981
'The Authority'	Local education authority
DES	Department of Education and Science
S.I.	Statutory Instrument
Secretary of State	Secretary of State for Education and Science
DES circulars	A circular issued by the Secretary of State for Education and Science. For the effect of these circulars see Ch. 1, n2.

DEFINITIONS AND TERMS

Parent — The natural parent, a guardian, and every person who has actual custody of the child or young person.[1]

Child — A person who is not over compulsory school age.

Compulsory School Age — Age 5–16, or more precisely, it begins at the beginning of the term after the child reaches the age of 5 and ends either at the end of the Spring term of the school year in which the child attains the age of the 16 if his birthday is between the 1 of September and the 30 January, or on the Friday before the last Monday in May if his birthday is after the end of January.

(Education Act 1944 as amended by the Revising of the School Leaving Age Order 1972 (S.I. 1972 444) and Section 9 of the Education Act 1962).

Warnock Report — Special Educational Needs —
Report of the Committee of Enquiry into the Education of Handicapped Children and Young People (HMSO Cmnd 7212).

Ordinary School — A school which is not a special school.

County School — A primary or secondary school maintained by a local education authority (or by a former authority)[2] or, a school which by virtue of any enactment repealed by the Education Act 1944 was deemed to be, or was treated, as a school provided by a former authority notwithstanding that it was not a school maintained by a former authority.

Notes

1. Education Act 1944 S 114 (1), as to the effect of this definition see the footnote n6 on page 47.

2. By section 114 (1) of the Education Act 1944 a 'former authority' means any authority which was a local education authority within the meaning of any enactment repealed by the Education Act 1944 or any earlier Act.

INTRODUCTION

The Education Act 1981 came into force on the 1st April 1983. In it, Parliament adopted many of the recommendations of the Warnock Committee.

The Warnock Committee was established in 1974 and the findings of the Committee were embodied in the Warnock Report (Cmnd. 7212)[1] which was presented to Parliament during May 1978. The terms of reference of the Warnock Committee were:

> To review educational provision in England, Scotland and Wales for children and young people handicapped by disabilities of body or mind, taking account of the medical aspects of their needs, together with arrangements to prepare them for entry into employment; to consider the most effective use of resources for these purposes; and to make recommendations.

The Warnock Report advocates a system of education whereby, so far as is possible, children suffering from all types of disability are educated in ordinary schools. The Education Act 1981 adopts this recommendation of the Warnock Committee insofar as Section 2 of the Act imposes a duty upon local education authorities to educate children with 'special educational needs' in ordinary schools. Prior to the Act such children were often 'labelled' as physically or mentally handicapped or educationally subnormal and many were educated in special schools.

The Warnock Committee argued that such children should, wherever possible, be fully integrated into ordinary schools; and that measures be taken to dispel the stigma attached to special schools, and to those who attend such schools. With these aims in mind, the Warnock Committee recommended that the concept of 'handicap' be substituted by that of 'special educational need' and, similarly, that the concept of 'special educational treatment' be replaced by the concept of 'special educational provision'. This new vocabulary has been adopted by Parliament in the Education Act 1981. The new terms are far wider than those they replace

11

and consequently many children will for the first time fall within the scope of the law relating to special education.

A primary concern of the Warnock Committee was the procedure by which children with special educational needs are identified and assessed. Both the Act and the regulations made pursuant to the powers conferred upon the Secretary of State for Education and Science by the Act, are designed to ensure that assessment be both thorough and continuous. The Act imposes a duty upon local education authorities to notify and consult the parent of any child who is to be assessed, and it is possible for any such parent who is dissatisfied with an assessment made in relation to his child to appeal to the Secretary of State. A local education authority may also be under a duty, in respect of certain of the children who are assessed, to prepare a written statement declaring the specific special educational needs of the child and the provision required to meet those needs. The provisions requiring local education authorities to prepare such a statement are particularly important since the Act imposes a duty upon the authority to arrange that the special educational provision specified in the statement is made for the child. A parent who is dissatisfied with the contents of the statement may appeal to a local appeals committee, and thereafter, to the Secretary of State.

It is hoped that this book will be of guidance to both those who seek to exercise their rights under the Act and also to those whose duty it is to implement its provisions and fulfil the duties it imposes — to welfare and education law practitioners, 'educationalists', and parents. Consequently, wherever necessary legal terms are explained. Because the Act, more than any other piece of Education legislation, encourages parental involvement in the education of children with special educational needs, there is a special emphasis on the appeal procedures available to those wishing either to challenge a breach of duty, or enforce a statutory right imposed by the Act. The appeal procedures, including 'school choice appeals' under the Education Act 1980, are the subject of detailed analysis in Chapter 11.

The appendices to this book contain a number of items of general importance including selected extracts from the Code of Practice on appeals to local committees which has been drafted by the Association of Metropolitan Authorities in consultation with the Council on Tribunals.

This book is intended to be an exposition of the 'law relating to special educational needs'. Consequently, to ensure a comprehensive coverage of the subject, where appropriate, reference is made to the Education Act 1944 and the Education Act 1980. Detailed reference is also made both to circulars issued by the Department of Education and Science[2] and to the regulations issued by the Secretary of State for Education and Science pursuant to the powers conferred upon him by the Education Act 1981.

The Law is stated as on the 1st March 1984.

I wish to thank Sue Goldthorp for typing the manuscript, and the controller of Her Majesty's Stationery Office for permission to use Crown copyright material.

Notes

1. *Special Educational Needs* Report of the Committee of Enquiry into the Education of Handicapped Children and Young People.

2. These circulars, issued by the Department of Education and Science, are intended to be of guidance to those administering the Act. Whilst they are in no sense legally binding the courts will, in appropriate cases, refer to them. They may in certain cases be persuasive as to what is reasonable.

1 THE MEANING OF SPECIAL EDUCATIONAL NEED

The Position Prior to the Education Act 1981

The term 'special educational need' is a creature of the Education Act 1981. It replaces the notion of 'special education treatment' which is embodied in the Education Act 1944. The Education Act 1944 requires that a local education authority, in fulfilling the duty imposed by Section 8(1) of that Act to secure that sufficient schools are available in its area for providing primary and secondary education, should have regard to a number of considerations. One of these considerations was the need to secure that provision was made for pupils suffering from any disability of mind or body by providing, either in special schools or otherwise, special educational treatment. Special educational treatment was defined as education by special methods appropriate for persons suffering from any disability of mind or body.

The law relating to special educational treatment was to be found in Section 33 and Section 34 of the Education Act 1944 and both of these sections were repealed by Section 21 of the Education Act 1981. Under Section 33(1) of the Education Act 1944 the Minister was endowed with the power to make regulations defining the categories[1] of pupils requiring special educational treatment. Section 33(2) ensured that children requiring special educational treatment would be segregated. It provided that the arrangements made by local education authorities for the special educational treatment of pupils should, so far as was practicable, provide for the education of pupils suffering from serious disabilities in special schools appropriate for the particular category of disability. Where the disability was not serious the local education authority had a choice as to whether such children were educated in special schools or in ordinary schools.

By Section 34 of the Education Act 1944 every local education authority was under a duty to ascertain which children in its area required special educational treatment. Under Section 34(1), after

15

giving due notice, a local education authority had the power to require the parent of any child over 2 years of age to submit the child for medical examination. The parent of any child of 2 years or over could request the local education authority to commission a medical examination for his child. The local education authority was bound to comply with any reasonable request. The parent of any child who was to be medically examined had the right to be notified and a right to be present at the examination. Further, the parent of a child who had been medically examined under the provisions of Section 34 had a right to be notified of the result of such examination.

Neither the Education Act 1944, nor the regulations made pursuant to it, made any provision as to how children were to be assessed prior to school placement and there was no duty to educate children in ordinary schools. Parents had no right to be consulted, there was no statutory appeals procedure through which a parent could challenge the decision of a local education authority, and a parent had no statutory right to have his child's educational needs assessed.

The Concept of Special Educational Need in the Education Act 1981

The concept of special educational need lies at the heart of the Education Act 1981, and its meaning is crucial to a proper understanding of the legislation. In accordance with the recommendations of the Warnock Committee, the draftsmen of the Education Act 1981 adopted the term 'special educational needs' and substituted it for that of 'special educational treatment'.[2] Section 1(1) of the Education Act 1981 provides that a child has special educational needs if '*he has a learning difficulty which calls for special educational provision to be made for him*'.

A 'child' is defined in Section 20 to include any person who has not attained the age of 19 years and is registered as a pupil at a school. This definition of special educational need includes two clauses which require explanation—

(1) 'learning difficulty' and
(2) 'special educational provision'.

Learning Difficulty

'Learning difficulty' is defined in Section 1(2) in these terms:

Subject to subsection (4) below, a child has a 'learning difficulty' if —

(a) he has a significantly greater difficulty in learning than the majority of children of his age; or

(b) he has a disability which either prevents or hinders him from making use of educational facilities of a kind generally provided in schools, within the area of the local authority concerned, for children of his age; or

(c) he is under the age of 5 years and is, or would be if special educational provision were not made for him, likely to fall within paragraph (a) or (b) when over that age.

The draftsmen of the Education Act 1981 were confronted with the difficulty of devising a definition of special educational need without resorting to a formal classification of needs. Such a classification, which would inevitably have been linked to causal factors, would have been contrary to the spirit of both the Warnock Report and of the legislation. The Warnock Committee gave detailed consideration to the sort of 'needs' experienced by children. At paragraph 3:38 of the Warnock Report special education is defined as encompassing 'the whole range and variety of additional help, whether it is provided on a full or part-time basis, by which children may be helped to overcome educational difficulties, however they are caused'. The Warnock Committee estimated that approximately 20 per cent of the nation's pupils might, at some time during their education, experience some form of special educational need. This estimate of the scale of special educational need appears to have been accepted both by Parliament, during the Parliamentary debate, and by the Secretary of State for Education and Science who at paragraph 3 of DES circular number 8/81 states:

Special educational needs may arise from a variety of causes, and the concept embraces a wider group of pupils than those at present formally ascertained as handicapped (approximately 2% of the school population). The Warnock committee estimated as an indication of scale that nationally 20% of pupils might have special educational needs at some time during their school careers. The proportion of children with such needs would however, vary from area to area and from school to school.

The definition of learning difficulty in Section 1 of the Education Act 1981 embraces a wide range of both short-term and long-term disability. The disability may, amongst other things, be mental, physical, behavioural, emotional or social. The effect of Section 1(2)(b) is to extend the definition to cover those children with physical disabilities. During the special standing committee stage in the House of Commons some concern was expressed regarding the effect of Section 1(2)(b) which, it was suggested, was to label a child with a minor physical disability as having a learning difficulty. It was argued that a consequence of this was that such a child could be treated as having special educational needs and, if necessary, placed in a special school. It is submitted that these fears were to some extent unwarranted for the definition of special educational need must be considered in conjunction with Section 2(2), Section 2(3) and Section 7 of the Act. The effect of Section 7 is that it is only open to a local authority to educate a child in a special school in circumstances where a statement is maintained in respect of the child. Section 2(2) and Section 2(3) provide that where a local education authority is under a duty to maintain a statement under Section 7 of the Act,[3] the local education authority will also be under a duty to educate such a child in an ordinary school. However, the local education authority will only be under such a duty if certain conditions are fulfilled.[4] Briefly, the conditions are that account has to be taken of the views of the child's parents and, secondly, educating the child in an ordinary school must be compatible with his receiving the special provision that he requires, the provision of efficient education for the children with whom he will be educated, and the efficient use of resources. It may of course be argued that to make special provision for a child with a minor physical disability is not an efficient use of resources, and certainly there must come a point where the making of certain provision by an authority may not be regarded as an efficient use of resources. However, whilst each case must depend upon its own facts, it is submitted that such an argument would not be tenable where only limited additional provision is required to meet a child's particular educational needs.

Section 1 of the Education Act 1981 contains a significant exception to the general definition of learning difficulty. Section 1(4) provides that a child is not to be taken as having a learning difficulty solely because the language (or form of a language) in which he is, or will be taught, is different from the language (or form of language) which has at anytime been spoken in his home. Consequently, the learning difficulty which is often widespread in areas where there is a large immigrant population, is excluded. It follows therefore that a local education authority is under no duty to provide special educational provision for such a child under the Education Act 1981 unless he also suffers from some other learning difficulty. However, local education authorities remain under a duty to consider the needs of such children when making general provision under Section 8 of the Education Act 1944.

There will be cases where it will be necessary to distinguish the effect of one learning difficulty from the effect of another and it remains to be seen just how far this will be possible. This particular difficulty is recognised by the Secretary of State who at paragraph 70 of DES Circular 1/83 states:

> LEAs may find it difficult to determine whether a child who is not yet fluent in the language of instruction may have special educational needs, and every attempt should be made in such a case to communicate with the child in a language with which he is conversant. In assessing the child's special educational needs, it is important to take account of the possibility that cultural differences may mask the child's true learning potential. . . .

Intelligence tests may be used, both to resolve this difficulty (and in relation to the general assessment of children). During the last decade American courts have been called upon to investigate the fairness of such tests. Some of these cases have involved the Wechsler Intelligence Scale for Children (WISC) and the Wechsler Intelligence Scale for Children — Revised (WISC-R) tests which are widely used in this country. These tests have been criticised on the grounds of cultural bias. The Education Act 1981 increases the likelihood of questions as to the validity of intelligence tests arising as collateral issues in the English courts, not only because it imposes a duty to educate children with special educational needs in ordinary schools (see Chapter 2) but also because the Act is intended to encourage parents to participate in the assessment procedures. In the past many children from ethnic minorities have been placed in special schools on the basis of intelligence tests. It could be argued that such children should be educated in an ordinary school. A parent may seek to demonstrate that a test which has been administered to his child is culturally biased against his child. Whilst in recent years there has been a spate of litigation in the American courts in relation to intelligence tests no pattern to the decisions has yet emerged. In *LARRY P. -v- RILES* (1979) intelligence tests were held to discriminate unfairly against black children in circumstances where they had been used to determine eligibility for special school placement in California. However in *PASE* (Parents in Action on Special Education) *-v- HANNON* (1980) it was held that intelligence tests are, in general, not discriminatory. The case was determined in favour of the defendants primarily because the plaintiff failed to discharge the burden of proof. In his judgment, Judge Grady said that a number of items on the WISC-R test might be discriminatory. For example, the Judge said that the question 'what is the colour of rubies?' could be criticised as confusing to black children since 'Ruby' is a common West Indian woman's name. Similarly, the question 'What is the thing to do if a boy/girl much smaller than yourself starts a fight with you?' was, in the opinion of the Judge, likely to invoke a much harsher response from a coloured youth.

'Special Educational Provision'

Special educational provision is defined in Section 1(3) of the Education Act 1981 as:

(a) in relation to a child who has attained the age of 2 years, educational provision which is additional to, or otherwise different from, the educational provision made generally for children of his age in schools maintained by the local education authority concerned; and

(b) in relation to any child under that age, educational provision of any kind.

It follows therefore that Section 1(3)(a) refers to any child aged between 2 and 18 inclusive. Section 1(3)(b) refers to any child under 2 years of age. The Act does not give any further guidance as to the meaning of special educational provision. However, it is submitted that it is implicit in Section 1(3) that special educational provision means provision over and above that provision usually made by the authority concerned. The inclusion of the words 'in schools maintained by the local education authority concerned' ensure that the test as to whether provision is 'special educational provision' is a subjective one referable to the authority concerned. Some further guidance on this point may be gleaned from paragraph 14 of DES circular 1/83.[5]

Notes

1. Such categories were defined in SI 1959 365. Handicapped Pupils and Special School Regulations.

2. See page 15.

3. See page 51 with regard to the effect of Section 7 of the Act and circumstances in which the local education authority must maintain a statement.

4. See page 24 for further discussion of the effect of Section 2(2) and Section 2(3) of the Act.

5. See page 37.

2 THE GENERAL DUTIES AFFECTING CHILDREN WITH SPECIAL EDUCATIONAL NEEDS UNDER THE EDUCATION ACT 1981

The Duty to have Regard to the Need for Securing Special Educational Provision

Section 8(2) of the Education Act 1944 requires local education authorities to have regard to certain matters in fulfilling their duty to secure provision of primary and secondary schools. We have seen that one of those matters was 'the need for securing that provision is made for pupils who suffer from any disability of mind or body by providing, either in special schools or otherwise, special educational treatment, that is to say, education by special methods appropriate for persons suffering from that disability'. This provision was repealed by Section 2(1) of the Education Act 1981 which substitutes the words 'to the need for securing that special educational provision is made for pupils who have special educational needs'.

The Duty to Educate Children in Ordinary Schools

In Chapter 4 it will be seen that in certain circumstances local education authorities are under a duty to provide a statement of a child's special educational needs. Such children may conveniently be referred to as 'statemented children'. Such a statement will include details of the special educational needs of the child together with the special educational provision required to meet those needs. Where a local education authority arranges special educational provision for a child for whom they maintain a statement under Section 7 of the Act it is the duty of the local education authority to secure that such a child is educated in an ordinary school rather than a special school. However, this duty to educate in ordinary schools only arises if two conditions are satisfied.

These conditions are referred to in Section 2(2) and Section 2(3) which provide that:

> (2) Where a local education authority arrange special educational provision for a child for whom they maintain a statement under Section 7 of this Act it shall be the duty of the authority, if the conditions mentioned in subsection (3) below are satisfied; to secure that he is educated in an ordinary school.
>
> (3) The conditions are that account has been taken, in accordance with Section 7, of the views of the child's parent and that educating the child in an ordinary school is compatible with —
>
>   (a) his receiving the special educational provision that he requires;
>   (b) that provision of efficient education for the children with whom he will be educated; and
>   (c) the efficient use of resources.

A curious feature of Sections 2(2) and 2(3) is that they are, in contrast to many of the provisions of the Act, expressed in objective language. It is therefore not simply a question of the local education authority satisfying itself as to whether educating the child in an ordinary school is, or is not, compatible with the objectives set out in Section 2(3). In other words the effect of Section 2(2) and Section 2(3) is that a local education authority would not be entitled simply to say 'this is our decision and there are reasonable grounds for reaching such a decision'.[1] The proper test appears to be an objective one, namely, have the conditions been complied with? However, the test will be subjective in the sense that, the question of whether educating the child in an ordinary school is compatible with the efficient use of resources, will be referable to the resources of the local education authority in question, and not those of the average, or any other, local education authority.[2]

Despite the inherent limitations of Sections 2(2) and 2(3), for the first time in the history of education, they place local education authorities under a duty to educate children with special needs in ordinary schools. It is clear that the spirit of the legislation is to ensure that, wherever possible, children with special needs are educated in ordinary schools and it is to be hoped that local education authorities will interpret Section 2(3) with this in mind.

Challenging a Local Education Authority's Decision in Relation to the Duty to Educate in Ordinary Schools

The method of challenging the decision of a local education authority in relation to the duty to educate in ordinary schools will depend upon whether or not there is a statement in existence. If a local education authority maintains a statement in relation to a child the parent may wish either:

(1) to challenge the decision of the local education authority to educate his child in an ordinary school (that is where the statement specifies that special provision be made for the child in an ordinary school); or
(2) to challenge a failure to educate his child in an ordinary school (for example, where the statement provides that the child is to be educated in a special school).

A parent wishing to challenge an alleged breach of the duty to educate his child in an ordinary school should do so by attacking the statement. Presumably, such a parent would argue that the school named in the statement was unsuitable. Consequently, a parent wishing to argue that his child should be educated in an ordinary school, rather than a special school, should seek to demonstrate that Section 2(3) is complied with. Conversely, a parent who wishes to argue that his child should be educated in a special school should argue that the Section 2(3) objectives have not been complied with.

The provisions in relation to the specific appeals procedures are discussed in detail in Chapter 11. However, stated briefly, an aggrieved parent should first lodge an appeal with the local appeals committee and then, if necessary, he should appeal to the Secretary of State.

A parent who remains dissatisfied may have grounds for applying for a 'judicial review' of the decision of the local education authority (see page 95). In order to succeed on an application for judicial review the parent would have to demonstrate that the local education authority have either erred in law or that the local education authority have reached a decision which no reasonable local education authority could have reached, for example, by taking into account matters which should not have been taken into account, or by failing to take matters into account which they ought properly to have taken into account.

Where the local education authority decide not to maintain a statement in relation to a child, a parent may appeal to the Secretary of State who may direct the local education authority to reconsider it's decision. If a local education authority decide to place a child in a special school without maintaining a statement, the decision to do so could be challenged by way of 'judicial review' on the grounds of unreasonableness since a special school is clearly special educational provision, and the local education authority would therefore be under a duty to maintain a statement in respect of the child.

The Duty to Integrate into Ordinary Schools

Section 2(7) of the Act provides that:

> Where a child who has special educational needs is being educated in an ordinary school maintained by a local education authority it shall be the duty of those concerned with making special educational provision for that child to secure, so far as is both compatible with the objectives mentioned in paragraphs (a) to (c) of subsection (3) above and reasonably practicable, that the child engages in the activities of the school together with children who do not have special educational needs.

Local education authorities are under a duty to 'integrate' children with special educational needs into ordinary schools so long as integration is compatible with the objectives mentioned in Section 2(3), namely, that such integration is compatible with the child receiving the special education that he requires, the provision of efficient education for the children with whom he will be educated, and the efficient use of resources (see page 24).

Further, the ambit of this duty is to be defined by what is 'reasonably practicable'. Apparently, what is 'reasonably practicable' is to be judged by the same standard as is the question of whether the objectives mentioned in Section 2(3) are met. In other words, the proper test is an objective one, applied to the local education authority in question. Has this local education authority reached the correct conclusion?

The Duty to Secure that Provision is Made

Section 2(5) of the Education Act 1981 provides:

> It shall be the duty of the governors, in the case of a county or voluntary school, and of the local education authority by whom the school is maintained, in the case of a maintained nursery school —
>
> (a) to use their best endeavours, in exercising their functions in relation to the school, to secure that if any registered pupil has special educational needs the special educational provision that is required for him is made;
>
> (b) to secure that, where the responsible person has been informed by the local education authority that a registered pupil has special educational needs, those needs are made known to all who are likely to teach him; and
>
> (c) to secure that the teachers in the school are aware of the importance of identifying, and providing for, those registered pupils who have special educational needs.

This subsection imposes three duties. All three duties are directed towards ensuing that special educational provision is made for the individual child.

Significantly, save in the case of maintained nursery schools, all three duties appertain to the governors and not to the local education authority. In one sense this is surprising since the governors do not determine the financial resources available to them, these are determined by the local education authority. By Section 2(5)(a) governors (and in the case of nursery schools, the local education authority) are directed to use their 'best endeavours' to ensure that special educational provision is made for pupils with special educational needs. The duty is not an absolute one. The governors are merely directed to use their 'best endeavours'. Presumably the expression 'best endeavours' really means 'best endeavours within the financial resources available' since the Act is not intended to have resource implications and since the governors do not determine the financial resources available to them.

This duty upon the governors to ensure that provision is made for each child with special educational needs should be distinguished from the duty under which local education authorities must secure that special educational provision is made for pupils who have special educational needs, (imposed by Section 2(1) of the Act). Unfortunately, the duty which is intended to ensure that provision be made for the individual child, namely that imposed by Section 2(5), is not as strict as that contained in Section 2(1) because, as we have seen, it merely directs the governors to use their 'best endeavours'. It will be difficult to establish a breach of such a duty expressed in such vague terms. Whether or not best endeavours have been made will depend upon the circumstances of each case but it is submitted that they should generally include either formal or informal instruction to teachers in relation to the importance of, and means by which, the identification and assessment of children with special educational needs may be effected; and the establishing of proper assessment and identification procedures.[3]

It is submitted that it is desirable, wherever possible, that governors should ensure that their schools make provision for the referral of particular children with special educational needs to a member of staff with special expertise in that field. Many local education authorities are now encouraging schools to appoint a member of staff, or in some cases the headmaster will himself assume the role, to have special responsibility for ensuring that all members of staff are aware of the effect of, and duties imposed by, the Education Act 1981. It is submitted that, wherever possible, governors should similarly be concerned in fulfilling the duties imposed upon them by Section 2(5).

Section 2(5)(b) and (c) are intended to ensure that the staff of schools with pupils who have special educational needs are aware of those needs; and that where the responsible person (in the case of county or voluntary schools the responsible person would usually be the head teacher or the chairman of the governors, and in the case of nursery schools the responsible person will be the head teacher) has been informed by the local education authority that such a pupil is registered at the school, those needs are made known to all who are likely to teach him.

Whilst the Act leaves the responsibility for ensuring that provision is made for the individual child entirely in the hands of the governors rather than the local education authority, it is clear from paragraph 6 of Circular 8/81 that the Secretary of State envisages a degree of co-operation between authorities and governors:

> The Secretary of State hopes that, as well as reviewing their arrangements for special educational provision as required by Section 2(4), L.E.As will exercise close oversight of arrangements made by the Governors of County and Voluntary Schools for identifying and providing for individual pupils' special educational needs in ordinary schools. In particular the Secretary of State hopes that L.E.As will encourage the early appointment of a responsible person in such schools in advance of the implementation of Section 2(5) of the Act.

The Duty to Review Special Educational Provision

The Education Act 1944 did not provide for the review of special educational provision. By Section 2(4) of the Education Act 1981:

> it shall be the duty of every local education authority to keep under review the arrangements made by them for special educational provision.

Whilst the Act does not provide any guidance as to the nature of the review envisaged, paragraph 6 of the Home Office Circular 8/81 (see page 28) may be interpreted as requiring that the review should include, amongst other things, overseeing arrangements made by governors pursuant to Section 2(5) of the Act. However, there is no statutory basis for this view.

Notes

1. As to the circumstances where a decision of an authority may be said to be unreasonable, albeit made in exercising a discretion, see page 95. If such a decision can properly be said to be 'unreasonable' judicial review may lie.
2. The interpretation of Sections 2(2) and 2(3) is further considered on page 92ff.
3. See page 32 for the duty upon local education authorities to identify the children in respect of whom they must determine the special educational provision required.

3 THE DUTIES RELATING TO THE IDENTIFICATION AND ASSESSMENT OF CHILDREN WITH SPECIAL EDUCATIONAL NEEDS

The Warnock Report

We have seen that it was estimated by the Warnock Committee that approximately 20 per cent of school children have special educational needs at some stage during their education. Indeed, the Warnock Committee were careful to note that whilst the special educational needs of some children might continue for relatively long periods, and in some cases permanently, those of other children may, if promptly and effectively met, cease to exist. With regard to this, the authors of the Warnock Report commented, 'this means that a teacher of a mixed ability class of 30, even in an ordinary school, should be aware that possibly as many as 6 of them may require some form of special educational provision at some time during their school life, and about 4 or 5 of them may require special educational provision at any given time'. The Warnock Committee was conscious of the wide variety of special educational need within this broad category consisting of 20 per cent of the school population. This group includes, amongst others, those children who have severe handicaps. The authors of the Warnock Report thus comment:

> We recognise that our recommendation that statutory categories of handicap should be abolished may give rise to concern about how to safeguard the interests of children with severe, complex and long-term disabilities. We have found ourselves on the horns of a dilemma. On the one hand we are aware that any kind of special resource or service for such children runs the risk of emphasising the idea of their separateness, an idea which we are anxious to dispel, and of limiting the notion of special education to the provision made for such children. On the other hand, unless an obligation is clearly placed on local education authorities to provide for the special needs of such children,

there is a danger that their requirement for specialist resources will be inadequately met . . . in order to resolve this difficulty, we have tried to devise a system which, while avoiding the disadvantages inherent in categorisation, will preserve the advantages which it confers. *We recommend that there should be a system of recording as in need of special educational provision those children, who, on the basis of a detailed profile of their needs prepared by a multi-professional team, are judged by their local education authority to require special educational provision not generally available in ordinary schools.*

It was estimated that approximately 2 per cent of the country's school population will require such 'recording'. Sections 4–7 of the Education Act 1981 give legislative force to the recommendations of the Warnock Committee relating to the assessment and identification of children with special educational needs.

The Duty to Identify

Section 4(1) of the Education Act 1981 provides that:

It shall be the duty of every local education authority to exercise their powers under this Act with a view to securing that, of the children for whom they are responsible, those with special educational needs which call for the local education authority to determine the special educational provision that should be made for them are identified by the authority.

This is the general duty to identify children having special educational needs such as to require special educational provision to be made for them. This provision relates to those children in respect of whom the local education authority maintain a statement in accordance with Section 7 of the Act. Consequently, Section 4(1) does not relate to all children with special educational needs, it merely relates to those whose needs are such as to require the local education authority to determine the special educational provision that should be made to meet those needs within the terms of Section 7 of the Act (see page 49ff). It follows therefore that this provision effectively relates to the category of children with severe complex and long-term disabilities which the Warnock Committee estimated would include approximately 2 per cent of the country's school children. This estimate has already had a profound effect both upon the way in which the Act has been interpreted by local education authorities and upon the numbers (in practice, the degree and types of disability) of children who local education authorities are treating as falling within the assessment provisions of the Act.

However, it is important to appreciate that the key to all the assessment and identification provisions of the Act, (Sections 4–10 inclusive) is to be found in Section 7. This is so with regard to Section 4, since Section 4 only applies to those children in respect of whom the local education authority determine the special educational provision under Section 7. Under Section 7, and this is the subject of detailed discussion in Chapter 4, local education authorities are only under a duty to determine the special educational provision to be made for a child if they are of 'the opinion' that they should 'determine' such provision. The Act is devoid of any guidelines as to the types of degrees of disability which fall within the ambit of 7.[1] In other words, local education authorities are given little help as to how they should arrive at their opinion under Section 7. It is clear that Section 7 is not intended to include all children with any educational needs whatsoever, and, in the absence of any judicial elucidation hitherto, local education authorities are seeking to derive what help they can both from the Warnock Report and from the DES circulars.

The duty imposed by Section 4(1) falls upon the local education authority and not upon the governors or the head teacher of particular schools responsible for such children. Presumably, the reason for this is that those involved in identifying children with special educational needs, doctors, educational psychologists etc., work as agents of the local education authority and not of particular schools.

The Meaning of 'Children For Whom the Local Education Authority are Responsible'

Section 4(1) applies to children for whom the local education authority are responsible. Whilst Sections 1–3 of the Act relate to all children with special educational needs (including children under 2 years of age) Section 4(1) does not apply to children under 2 years of age. The meaning of the expression 'children for whom they are responsible' contained in Section 4(1) is defined in Section 4(2):

> For the purposes of this Act a local education authority are responsible for a child if he is in their area and —
> (a) he is registered as a pupil at a school maintained by them or is registered as a pupil in pursuance of arrangements made by them by virtue of Section 6 of the Education (Miscellaneous Provisions) Act 1953 at a school which is not maintained by them or another local education authority; or
> (b) he has been brought to their attention as having, or as probably having, special educational needs and —
>   (i) is registered as a pupil at a school but does not fall within paragraph (a) above; or
>   (ii) is not registered as a pupil at a school and is not under the age of 2 years or over the compulsory school age.

This is an important definition because it is incorporated into both Section 5 (which provides for the assessment of children with special educational needs) (see page 36) and Section 7 (which provides that 'the local education authority who are responsible for the child shall, if they are of the opinion that they should determine the special educational provision that should be made for him, make a statement of his special educational needs') (see page 49). A child will fall within this definition if he is 'in the area'; it does not appear to be necessary that the child is residing in the area for which the local education authority is responsible. Section 4(2)(a) includes, in addition to children who are over 2 years of age and under 19 years of age who are registered as pupils at maintained schools, those children who are not registered at schools maintained by the local education authority but whose educational provision has been arranged by the local education authority at non-maintained schools, (such children must also be 2 years of age or over and under 19 years of age). Section 4(2)(b) also applies to children 2 years of age or over but under 19 years of age. Section 4(2)(b) extends the definition of a child for whom the local education authority will be responsible to include a child who is living in the area in respect of which the local education authority are responsible for education, but who is registered at a school which does not fall within those schools included in Section 4(2)(a). In particular, Section 4(2)(b)(i) extends the definition to include those children registered at non-maintained schools but who have not been placed there pursuant to the powers conferred upon local education authorities by Section 6 of the Education (Miscellaneous Provision) Act 1953.[2] Section 4(2)(b)(i) applies to children 2 years of age or over but under 19 years of age. Section 4(2)(b)(ii) extends the definition to include children who are not registered at any school but who are 'in' the area for which the local education authority is responsible. However, such a child will only fall within the definition if he is over 2 years of age and under 16 years of age.

The Duty to Assess

The Warnock Report

We have seen that the Warnock Committee recommended the introduction of a system of 'recording' the special educational needs (and special educational provision required to meet those needs) of children (see pages 31–32). Proper assessment is a prerequisite of such a system. The view of the Warnock Committee was that:

> Enforceable procedures will continue to be needed, in circumstances where parents believe that their child has special educational needs, which are not recognised by the authority, or where the authority considers that a child has special educational needs which the parents do not accept. The statutory procedure should embody two features which we regard as indispensable: first, in line with our view that the need for special education may begin at birth the procedures should be applicable to any child from birth, and secondly, the multi-professional nature of effective assessment to which we draw attention in later paragraphs requires that the procedures should not be restricted to a medical examination alone. *We therefore recommend that Section 34 of the Education Act 1944 . . . should be amended to give local education authorities the power to require the*

*multi-professional assessment of children at any age (after due
notice to parents) and to impose on them a duty to comply with a
parental request for such assessment.*

This passage from the Warnock Report refers to two 'indispensable' features of a system of assessment. The first, that assessment should begin at birth, has not been adopted by the legislature since Section 5 applies to a child for whom a local education authority is responsible. We have seen that a local education authority will be responsible for a child if the child falls within the definition of responsibility contained in Section 4(2) — see pages 33–34 — of the Act. The second 'indispensable feature' of a system of assessment was said by the Warnock Committee to be 'the multi-professional nature of effective assessment'. This recommendation has been adopted by Parliament, and the Education (Special Educational Needs) Regulations 1983 (S.I. 1983 No: 29) makes detailed provision for the assessment of children with special educational needs.

The Duty

Section 5(1) of the Education Act 1981 provides that:

Where, in the case of a child for whom a local education authority are responsible, the authority are of the opinion —
  (a) That he has special educational needs which call for the authority to determine the special educational provision that should be made for him; or
  (b) That he probably has such special educational needs;
they shall make an assessment of his educational needs under this section.

The duty to assess children with special educational needs applies to children 'for whom the local authority are responsible'.[3] It is sufficient that a child falls within either Section 5(1)(a) or Section 5(1)(b). The decision as to whether or not to assess is one in which the local education authority has a discretion. The decision of the local education authority will be unimpeachable so long as it is a decision which is made upon reasonable grounds (see Chapter 11).

On one view the word 'probably' in Section 5(1) implies that the duty to assess only arises if it is more likely than not that the child has special educational needs. However, the duty to assess has been explained in broader terms by the Secretary of State in paragraph 13 of the DES circular 1/83 which states that 'formal procedures' should be initiated where there are 'prima facie grounds to suggest that a child's needs are such as to require provision additional to, or otherwise different from, the facilities and resources generally available in ordinary schools in the area under normal arrangements'. Paragraph 14 of DES circular 1/83 gives further guidance as to the meaning of 'additional' provision:

> The deciding factors in determining what constitutes additional or otherwise different provision are likely to vary from area to area depending on the range of provision normally available in an authority's schools. As a general rule, the Secretary of State expects LEA's to afford the protection of a statement to all children who have severe or complex learning difficulties which require the provision of extra resources in ordinary schools, a special school, a non-maintained special school, or an independent school approved for the purpose.

It is important to appreciate that the duty to assess under Section 5 of the Act only arises if the authority is of the opinion that the child has, or probably has, such special educational needs as require that the authority determine the special educational provision that should be made for the child. In other words, the duty to assess only arises where the authority are, or probably are, under a duty to prepare a statement pursuant to Section 7. To this extent Section 7 is the key to Section 5 and reference should be made to Chapter 4 for the circumstances in which a statement should be maintained.

Parental Requests and Mandatory Re-assessment

Section 9 of the Education Act 1981 provides that:

(1) If the parent of the child for whom a local education authority are responsible but for whom no statement is maintained by the authority under Section 7 asks the

authority to arrange for an assessment to be made of the child's educational needs, the authority shall comply with the request unless it is in their opinion unreasonable.

(2) If the parent of a child for whom a local education authority maintain a statement under Section 7 asks the authority to arrange an assessment of his educational needs under Section 5 and such an assessment has not been made within the period of 6 months ending with the date on which the request is made, the authority shall comply with the request unless they are satisfied that an assessment would be inappropriate.

Section 9 is an important provision. It gives the parent of a child the power to request that a local education authority undertake an assessment of his child's educational needs, even in circumstances where the local education authority have reasonably concluded that the child does not fall within the provisions of Section 5. The circumstances in which a parent may request an assessment of his child's educational needs by the local education authority are twofold.

1. Where the Local Educational Authority do not Maintain a Statement. In relation to assessment under Section 9(1) the Secretary of State at paragraph 21 of DES circular 8/81 states:

the assessment need not, however, be an assessment under Section 5 if the local education authority are satisfied, as a result of examining the child, that his special educational needs can be met without the need for a statement.

It is submitted that this statement is in one sense misleading. Clearly, if the local education authority are of the view that the child's special educational needs can be met without the need for an assessment any subsequent assessment would not be made pursuant to Section 5. Such an assessment would be made pursuant to Section 9(1). It is submitted that such an assessment should be made in the same way, with the same care, and subject to the same procedures and enquiries as if it had been made pursuant to Section 5. Section 9 contains nothing to suggest that the nature of the assessment for which it provides is to differ in any way from that which must be carried out pursuant to Section 5. It is submitted that both sections provide that the same exercise be undertaken (but in different circumstances); and had that not been the intention of Parliament a different view would have been expressed in the clearest possible terms.

Section 9(1) applies to all children in respect of whom the local education authority do not maintain a statement. Presumably, the parent of any such child may call for an assessment of his child, whether the child has special educational needs or not. The only caveat to this is that the request must not, 'in the opinion' of the local education authority, be unreasonable. This, of course, begs the question as to when a request will be unreasonable. It is submitted that Section 9(1) should be understood as providing that, pursuant to a parental request, an assessment should be carried out in circumstances where the local education authority would not otherwise (in the absence of such a request) deem an assessment necessary under Section 5(1). Section 9(1) should be considered in the light of Section 5(1), so that where a local education authority have decided not to assess a child in accordance with Section 5(1) (in other words that it is of the opinion that the child does not have, or it is not probable that he has, special educational needs requiring the local education authority to determine the special educational provision that should be made for him), the authority should then consider whether or not a parental request for an assessment (assuming that a parental request has been made) is reasonable. A request will be unreasonable if it is one which no parent acting reasonably would make.[4] Local education authorities are given some guidance as to how to approach Section 9(1) in paragraph 22 of DES circular 8/81 which states that: 'an authority will only be able to refuse a request for an assessment under Section 9(1) if it is a request that no parent acting reasonably would make and the Secretary of State will normally expect local education authorities to comply with the request'.

2. Where the Local Education Authority Maintain a Statement in Respect of the Child. Section 9(2) provides for the situation where the local education authority maintain a statement of a child's special educational needs within the terms of Section 7 of the Act.[5] In these circumstances, a local education authority must (if requested) and such an assessment has not been made within the period of 6 months ending with the date on which the request was made, provide an assessment of the child's special educational needs. We have seen that Section 9(1) permits a local education authority to refuse a request if it considers such a request unreasonable. The caveat to Section 9(2) is expressed in broader terms because it provides that the local education authority may refuse a request under Section 9(2) where it is satisfied that an assessment would be 'inappropriate'. Paragraph 22 of DES circular 8/81 states that: 'Authorities will have more discretion to refuse a request to which Section 9(2) applies.' It is submitted that this must be correct.

Regulation 9 of the Educational (Special Educational Needs) Regulations 1983 (SI 1983 No: 29) provides for mandatory re-assessment where local education authorities maintain a statement in respect of a child whose educational needs have not been assessed since before he attained the age of 12 years and 6 months. In these circumstances the local education authority must carry out an assessment during the period of 12 months beginning with the day on which the child attained the age of 13 years and 6 months. The purpose of such mandatory assessment is to ensure that the child receives appropriate provision to equip him for employment.

The Procedure

Section 5(3) provides that where a local education authority propose to assess the educational needs of a child they must only do so after following the procedure specified by the section which provides that notice should be served upon the child's parent[6] informing him:

(1) That they propose to make an assessment;
(2) Of the procedure to be followed in making it;
(3) Of the name of the officer of the authority from whom further information may be obtained; and
(4) Of his right to make representations, and submit written evidence to the authority within such period (which shall not be less than 29 days beginning with the date on which the notice is served) as may be specified in the notice.

The DES circular 1/83 provides that the notice served upon the child's parent should be in the language with which the child's parents are familiar, or, failing that, a language for which they could readily obtain an interpreter. The Act does not contain a definition of service but Section 21(2) of the Act provides that it is to be construed as one with the principal Act, and Section 113 of the principal Act provides that a notice is deemed to be served if sent by pre-paid post to the last known place of residence.

Section 5(4) provides that after a local education authority have served such a notice upon the parent of the child and the 'period' specified in the notice has expired, the authority shall, if they consider it appropriate, after taking into account any representations made and evidence submitted to them in response to the notice, assess the educational needs of the child concerned.

It is submitted that the period specified in the notice may not, in any circumstances, be waived. This is so, even if the parent indicates, before the expiry of any such period that he does not wish to make any representations concerning his child.

Advice to be Sought Prior to an Assessment

The matters to be considered in making an assessment pursuant to Section 5 of the Act have been specified by the Secretary of State and are embodied in the Education (Special Educational Needs) Regulations 1983 (SI 1983 No:29). Regulation 4 provides that:

(1) For the purpose of making an assessment an education authority shall, in the case of the child concerned, seek —
   (a) Educational advice as provided in Regulation 5;
   (b) Medical advice as provided in Regulation 6;
   (c) Psychological advice as provided in Regulation 7; and
   (d) Any other advice which the authority consider desirable in the case in question for the purpose of arriving at a satisfactory assessment, subject however, to Regulation 12. [Regulation 12 makes special provision for children moving from one education area to another].[7]
(2) The advice sought in pursuance of Paragraph (1) shall be written advice relating to —
   (a) the educational, medical, psychological or other features of the case (according to the nature of the advice sought)

which appear to be relevant to the child's educational needs (including his likely future needs);

(b) how those features could affect the child's educational needs; and

(c) the provision rendered requisite by those features of the child's case, whether by way of special educational provision or non-educational provision additional thereto requisite if the child is properly to benefit therefrom.

Any person consulted in relation to Regulation 4(1) should be furnished with copies of representations made by the parent and any evidence submitted by or at the request of the parent. Any person so consulted may consult with further persons if it appears to him expedient to do so.

The Regulations give detailed instructions as to the educational, medical and psychological advice to be sought pursuant to Regulation 4(1). In paragraph 23 of DES circular 1/83 the Secretary of State gives some general guidance as to the considerations to which professional advisors should have regard when giving advice:

In order to promote the adoption of a common approach to advice on special educational needs, the Secretary of State recommends that each professional advisor should aim to give the appropriate professional view of the child's needs in terms of:

(i) the relevant aspects of the child's functioning, including his strengths and weaknesses, his relation with his environment at home and at school, and any relevant aspects of the child's past history;

(ii) the aims to which provision for the child should be directed to enable him to develop educationally and increase his independence;

(iii) the facilities and resources recommended to promote the achievement of these aims.

The educational advice should be sought from a qualified teacher. Such a person may be either:

(a) The head teacher of a school which the child has attended at some time within the preceding 18 months (if the head teacher has not himself taught the child within the preceding 18 months, he may give such advice after consultation with a teacher who has so taught the child), or

(b) If advice cannot be obtained from the head teacher, it may be obtained from a person whom the education authority are satisfied has experience of teaching children with special educational needs, or knowledge of the differing provision which may be called for in different cases to meet those needs.

If it appears to the local education authority that a child in question is deaf (or partially hearing) or blind (or otherwise visually handicapped) and the person from whom advice is sought is not qualified to teach deaf, or as the case may be, blind pupils, then the advice sought shall be advice given after consultation with a person who is so qualified.[8]

The medical advice referred to in Regulation 4 is to be sought from a fully registered medical practitioner who is either designated, for the purposes of the regulations, by the District Health Authority or is nominated by them.

The psychological advice referred to in Regulation 4 must be sought from either

(a) A person regularly employed by the education authority as an educational psychologist[9] or;

(b) From a person, in the case in question, engaged by the education authority as an educational psychologist.

Neither the legislation, nor the regulations, give any special place to psychological advice as against the other advice which local education authorities are required to seek. This represents a departure from past practice. Further, psychologists are given no guidelines as to the methods and practices to be used in reaching their conclusions and rendering their advice. The absence of clear directives has given rise to a divergence of opinion, particularly between on the one hand those who favour a curriculum-related approach to assessment and, on the other hand, those who prefer to rely upon the use of psychometric tests. It is possible to raise arguments to support both approaches. The whole tenor of the legislation with its emphasis on integrating those children with special educational needs into ordinary schools requires precise information as to a child's specific abilities.[10] It is said that such information can best be provided by a curriculum-related approach. However, Section 1(2) of the Act defines a child as having a learning difficulty if he has a 'significantly greater difficulty in learning than the majority of children of his age'. This definition of learning difficulty, which is the fundamental ingredient of special educational need, seems to require a measurement of the child's abilities which is relative to those of other children. It is said by those who favour psychometric assessment, that psychometric tests are best suited to provide such information.

However, psychologists have a wide discretion as to the methods of psychological assessment they employ. Neither approach to psychological assessment is precluded by the legislation or regulations, and so long as local education authorities behave reasonably and within the law they will not be open to correction from the courts. For detailed comment as to the grounds upon which a local education authority's decision may be open to challenge in the courts reference should be made to Chapter 11. Some examples of instances where a reliance upon psychological assessment might be regarded by the court as 'unreasonable' are —

Where a psychometric test has been administered to a child with a hearing difficulty; or
Where the sole basis of assessment is a psychometric test administered to a child at a time of emotional trauma.

An example of an instance where a court might rule that a local education authority has behaved illegally is if the psychological advice is given by a person who is not employed or engaged by the local education authority as an educational psychologist, and is therefore given in breach of paragraph 7 of the Education (Special Educational Needs) Regulations, 1983.

Neither the legislation nor the regulations specify whose task it should be to collate the advice which is elicited from the various specialist advisers. Many local education authorities have assumed that this should be undertaken by educational psychologists. However, some have appointed administrators to do this. Whilst this may be undesirable, there is no legal reason why this function should not be in the hands of administrators.

It is however clear that the ultimate responsibility for assessing the child's special educational needs rests with the local education authority. Paragraph 39 of DES circular 1/83 states:

Where there is a conflict in the professional advice submitted to the L.E.A., or where it is clear that further consideration is required to lead to a full understanding of the child's special educational needs, the L.E.A. should arrange further discussions among the professional advisers to arrive at the resolution of any conflict or uncertainty about the child's needs. Where it has not proved possible to reconcile differences in the advice submitted to the L.E.A. by their professional advisers, it will be for the L.E.A. as part of their assessment of the child's needs, to decide on the weight to be given to different kinds of advice.

In addition to considering the evidence submitted in accordance with Regulation 4, the local education authority, by virtue of Regulation 8, must also consider:

(1) any representations made by the child's parent;
(2) any evidence submitted by, or at the request of, that parent; and
(3) any information relating to the health or welfare of the child furnished by, or on behalf of, any District Health Authority or any Social Services Authority.

The Warnock Committee envisaged that there might be circumstances where residential assessment would be desirable. Neither the legislation nor the regulations make any provision for such assessment.

Examination of Children. Schedule 1 to the Education Act 1981 provides that a local education authority may serve a notice[11] upon a parent that his child is to be assessed and requiring the child's attendance for examination in accordance with the provisions of the notice. The parent of such a child shall be entitled to be present at the examination if he so desires. The notice should state the purpose of the examination, the time and place at which the examination is to be held, the name of the officer of the authority from whom further information may be obtained, inform the parent that he may submit such information to the authority as he may wish, and inform the parent of his right to be present at the examination. Any parent on whom such a notice has been served who fails, without reasonable excuse, to comply with it shall, if the notice relates to a child who was not over compulsory school age at the time stated in the notice as the time for holding the examination, be guilty of an offence and be liable on summary conviction to a fine not exceeding £50.

Assessing Children under 2 Years of Age

Section 5 does not apply to children under 2 years of age. By virtue of Section 6 of the Education Act 1981 a local education authority may, in relation to a child under 2 years of age, with the consent of the child's parent, make an assessment of the child's educational needs. Before making such assessment the local education authority must satisfy itself that either

(1) The child has special educational needs which call for the authority to determine the special educational provision that should be made for him, or;

(2) That he probably has such special educational needs.

If either of these conditions is fulfilled, and if the local education authority are requested to make such an assessment by the child's parent, the section provides that the local education authority 'shall' do so. Such an assessment may be made in such a manner as the local education authority considers appropriate. After making such an assessment the local education authority may make a statement of the child's special educational needs, and maintain that statement, in such manner as they consider appropriate. Once a statement has been made pursuant to Section 6 it will be open to review and challenge in the same way as any other statement.

Challenging an Assessment

The procedures through which an aggrieved parent may challenge an assessment of his child's special educational needs (or indeed, a failure to assess) are discussed in detail in Chapter 11.[12] Section 5 specifically provides that if, after making an assessment of the educational needs of a child under Section 5, the local education authority decide that they are not required to determine the special educational provision that should be made for him the parent may appeal in writing to the Secretary of State. Upon such an appeal, the Secretary of State may, if he thinks fit, direct the local education authority to reconsider their decision. However, the Secretary of State has no power to compel the local education authority to change its decision.

Notes

1. See pages 49ff. as to circumstances in which local education authorities must maintain a statement.
2. The Education (Miscellaneous Provisions) Act 1953 (Section 6) empowers local education authorities to make arrangements for the education of pupils in independent schools and pay their fees.
3. For the meaning of 'child for whom a local education authority are responsible' see page 33.
4. As to challenging a decision of a local education authority which a parent considers to be unreasonable see Chapter 11.
5. See Chapter 4 as to the circumstances in which a statement must be maintained.
6. Throughout the Act reference is made to 'parent' rather than 'parents' (see the definition of 'parent' in the table of definitions and terms). It is clear that, in certain instances in relation to a given child, two or more persons living at different addresses may fall within the definition of parent, it is submitted that in these circumstances references to 'parent' should be understood to mean all those persons falling within the definition of parent since the Act gives no guidance as to which particular person should be treated as the parent (for example, where the parents of a child are separated, both parents should be served with a notice issued under Section 5(3) of the Act).
7. The words in square parenthesis have been interpellated by the author and are not part of the Regulation.
8. 'Qualified teacher' means a person who in pursuance of the regulations relating to the employment of teachers (a) from time to time in force under Section 27 of the Education Act 1980 and (b) is qualified to be employed as a teacher at a school to which that Section applies.

A person qualified to teach deaf or blind pupils is a reference to a person who is so qualified to be employed at such a school as a teacher of a class for deaf, or as the case may be, blind pupils. (Otherwise than to give instruction in craft, trade or domestic subject.)
9. If the educational psychologist concerned believes that another psychologist has relevant knowledge or information relating to the child he should consult that other psychologist.

10. See reference to paragraph 23 of DES circular 1/83 on page 42.

11. For the meaning of service see page 42.

12. As to specific examples of the grounds upon which a psychological assessment may be challenged see page 44.

4 THE DUTY TO STATEMENT CHILDREN WITH SPECIAL EDUCATIONAL NEEDS

The Nature of the Duty

Section 7(1) provides that:

> Where an assessment has been made in respect of a child under Section 5, the local education authority who are responsible for the child shall, if they are of the opinion that they should determine the special educational provision that should be made for him, make a statement of his special educational needs and maintain that statement in accordance with the following provisions of this Act.

We have seen that the Warnock Committee recommended that there should be a system of 'recording as in need of special educational provision those children who, on the basis of a detailed profile of their needs prepared by a multi-professional team, are judged by their local education authority to require special educational provision not generally available in ordinary schools' (see page 31). Section 7 therefore gives effect to this recommendation and is primarily concerned with those children with severe, complex and long-term disabilities. It will be recalled that a local education authority are under a duty to assess a child if the authority are of the opinion, either that a child has special educational needs which call for the authority to determine the special educational provision that should be made for him, or if a child probably has such special educational needs. If, after assessment has been made, it transpires that the local education authority are of the opinion that they should determine the special educational provision that should be made for him they must make a statement of his special educational needs and maintain that statement in accordance with the provisions of Section 7 of the Education Act 1981. The relationship between Section 7 and the other assessment and identification provisions of the Act is

49

discussed on page 33. Section 7 applies to those children for whom the local education authority is responsible as defined by Section 4(2) of the Act (see page 33).

Whilst the Warnock Committee estimated that the proportion of children with severe, complex and long-term disabilities amounted to approximately 2 per cent of the child population, the numbers of children who will in fact be statemented will depend upon how the local education authorities, and ultimately, the courts, interpret the provisions of Section 7. Paragraph 9 of the DES circular 8/81 advises local education authorities in these terms —

The Secretary of State will expect local education authorities to afford children the protection of a statement of their special educational needs in all circumstances where extra resources in terms of staffing or equipment would be required to cater for those needs in an ordinary school. It is expected that the number will correspond approximately to those children formerly ascertained as handicapped under Section 34 of the 1944 Act.

Paragraph 14 of DES circular 1/83(ii), further advises that:

as a general rule, the Secretary of State expects local education authorities to afford the protection of a statement to all children who have severe or complex learning difficulties which require the provision of extra resources in ordinary schools, and in all cases where the child is placed in a special unit attached to an ordinary school.

Paragraph 15 of the circular states that 'formal procedures are not required where ordinary schools provide special educational provision from their own resources in the form of additional tuition or remedial provision, or, in normal circumstances, where the child attends a reading centre or unit for disruptive pupils'. However, it is submitted that such additional facilities, whether they are provided out of school's resources or not, are capable of falling within the definition of special educational provision contained in Section 1 of the Act, that is, 'provision not made generally for children . . . in schools, maintained by the local education authority'. The important question is whether the provision is made generally by the authority concerned.

One indication of the number of children who should be statemented pursuant to Section 7 of the Act is to be found in the transitional provisions to the Act which provide that during the 12 months following the legislation coming into force local education authorities should statement all those children currently in special schools. Such children amount to approximately 2 per cent of the present school population. Further, it is submitted that it is arguable that after the transitional period has lapsed (after 1 April 1984) a decision of a local authority not to maintain a statement in respect of a child who prior to the coming into force of the legislation (1 April 1983) was in a special school would be open to challenge in the Courts by way of judicial review (see Chapter 11). It is submitted that the transitional provisions are a clear indication that it was intended by parliament that local education authorities should maintain a statement in respect of, as a minimum, children who, prior to 1 April 1983, were in special schools, and that it would be unreasonable if such children were not to be made the subject of statements.

Whilst, as we have seen, any parent may, by reason of Section 9, request that the local education authority make an assessment of his child's educational needs there is no comparable provision enabling a parent to request that his child be statemented. Where a statement has been made in accordance with Section 7 of the Education Act 1981, it is the duty of the local education authority, unless the child's parent has made suitable arrangements, to arrange that the special educational provision specified in the statement is made for the child concerned. Consequently, the existence of the statement will ensure that the child's special educational needs are met. Further, it will help to ensure a continuity in the special educational provision made for children moving from one area to another (see page 55).

The Procedure

The preparation of a statement involves two stages which may be conveniently termed 'proposed statement' and the 'completed statement'. Prior to making a statement a local education authority must serve[1] upon the parent of the child concerned a copy of the proposed statement and a written notice explaining the parent's right to challenge the statement.[2]

Section 7 is designed to encourage parental involvement. At first sight the provisions of Section 7 of the Act which govern parental involvement in the statementing procedures appear dauntingly complex. Appendix 1 to this book is a flow chart showing the various stages of possible parental involvement in the making of a statement. It is possible to discern two 'courses' of parental intervention. Whilst these 'courses' may be considered in isolation from each other, they are not expressed in the statute to be in the alternative and accordingly a parent may follow either or both.

Course One

Upon receipt of a 'proposed statement' the parent may require the local education authority to arrange a meeting between himself and an officer of the authority at which the content of the 'proposed statement' can be discussed.[3] Such a meeting may be called within 15 days beginning on the date on which the proposed statement was served on the parent. If the parent is content with the outcome of such a meeting that will be an end to the matter. However, a parent who disagrees with the outcome of the meeting may, within 15 days of the date fixed for the first meeting, require the authority to arrange one or more meetings.[4] If a parent makes such a request the local education authority must arrange such meeting or meetings as they consider will enable the parent to discuss the relevant advice with the appropriate person or persons. Presumably therefore if the local education authority reasonably believe that a further meeting would be unnecessary and would serve no useful purpose they could refuse to call a further meeting. 'Relevant advice' means 'such of the advice given to the authority in connection with the assessment as they consider to be relevant to that part of the assessment with which the parent disagrees'. The 'appropriate person' is defined as 'the person who gave the relevant advice or any other person who, in the opinion of the authority, is the appropriate person to discuss it with the parent'. This definition of the 'appropriate person' requires that the local education authority determine the person. However, their opinion must be one which is reasonably held, and, generally speaking, it is assumed that a meeting requested under Section 7 should be with the person responsible for providing the information upon which the disputed matters in the statement have been based.

The Secretary of State has given some guidance as to when interviews should be called. Paragraph 15 of the DES circular 8/81 states that:

> the Secretary of State regards the parents right of interview with those concerned in assessment as a measure which will rarely need to be invoked if parents have been properly involved in the earlier stages of assessment. However, where a parent continues to have doubts about the appropriateness of the educational provision to be made for his child, the Secretary of State hopes that local education authorities will arrange meetings as quickly as possible to enable such a parent to have his questions answered.

Course Two

Section 7(4)(a) provides that a parent may make representations (or further representations) to the authority about the content of a proposed statement. Such representations should be made within 15 days beginning on the date on which the proposed statement was served[5] upon the parent. However, if in addition to making representations, the parent has also requested meetings with the local education authority (in other words, if a parent is also pursuing Course One) the Section 7(4)(a) representations must be made within the period of 15 days beginning with the date fixed for the last of those meetings.

The local education authority must consider all representations made to them, and notify the parents in writing of their decision. The local education authority will have three options open to them in reaching that decision. They may retain the statement in its original form, modify it, or determine not to make a statement. In addition to serving the statement on the parent the authority must supply the parent with notice in writing of his rights under the Education Act 1981 to appeal to the Secretary of State against the special educational provisions specified in the statement.[6] The parent must also be notified in writing of the name of the person to whom he may apply for information and advice about the child's special educational needs. The Act does not specify who that person should be.

Content of the Statement

Part 2 of the first schedule to the Education Act 1981 provides that a statement shall be in the prescribed form[7] and contain the prescribed information, in particular, it should:

(a) Give details of the authority's assessment of the special educational needs of the child; and

(b) specify the special educational provision to be made for the purpose of meeting those needs.

In exercising the powers conferred upon the Secretary of State under the Education Act 1981, the Secretary of State has now issued a 'prescribed form' which appears in the schedule to the Education (Special Educational Needs) Regulations 1983 (SI 1983 No: 29). This 'prescribed form' is widely used by local education authorities and is included in the appendices to this book. Some general guidance as to what should be included in the statement is to be found in Regulation 10, subsection (1), of the Education (Special Educational Needs) Regulations, 1983 (SI 1983 No: 29) which provides that:

A statement of a child's Special educational needs made in pursuance of Section 7(1) of the Act of 1981, shall also:

(a) Specify the special educational provision (in terms of facilities and equipment, staffing arrangements, curriculum or otherwise) which the education authority consider appropriate to meet those needs;

(b) Without prejudice to the generality of subparagraph (a), specify either:

   (i) the type of school which the education authority consider would be appropriate for the child, and if they consider that a particular school would be so appropriate, the name of that school, or

   (ii) if they consider it appropriate that the child should be provided with education otherwise than at a school, particulars of the provision which they consider would be appropriate;

(c) Specify any additional non-educational provision —

    (i) which, unless proposed to be made available by the education authority, they are satisfied will be made available by a District Health Authority, a Social Services Authority or some other body; and

    (ii) of which, in their opinion, advantage should be taken if the child is properly to benefit from the special educational provision specified in pursuance of subparagraph (a) and (b) above, and

(d) set out the representations, evidence, advice and information taken into consideration in pursuance of Regulation 8.[8]

Whilst of course the statement must comply with Regulation 10 there is no necessity that it follow precisely the 'prescribed form'. However, the regulations provide that it should be either set out in the 'prescribed form' or a 'form to the like effect'. The statement should be authenticated by the signature of a duly authorised officer of the education authority concerned.

The 'annex' to the DES circular 1/83 comprises a check list of the points to be considered by professional advisers in assessing a child's special educational needs. It is not expected that each professional adviser should consider all the matters contained in the annex, but it is hoped that each specialist will consider those matters which relate to his specialisation. The circular list is included in the appendices to this book.

The provisions relating to the disclosure to parents of reports, other than those which are annexed to the statement, are assessed and discussed in Chapter 12.

Children Moving from One Education Authority to Another

Where a child, in respect of whom a statement is maintained, moves from the area governed by one education authority to that governed by another, the erstwhile authority must transfer the statement to the new authority at the request of the new authority. The new authority should determine whether or not the conditions specified in Section 5(1) of the Act (see page 36ff.) are satisfied. If the local education authority decide that the conditions are not satisfied they must notify the child's parent that they are of that opinion and accordingly that they do not propose to make an assessment. However, if the new local education authority decide that the conditions specified in Section 5(1) are satisfied and serve[9] notice upon the child's parent that they propose to make an assessment, they may do so. Where the transferred statement was made within the period of 3 years immediately preceding the date of the notice, with the written agreement of the parent, the educational, medical or psychological advice which the new authority are required to seek by Regulation (4)1) (see page 41) may be sought from the old authority instead of as provided in the Education (Special Educational Needs) Regulations 1983 (SI 1983 No: 29). In such cases, any reference in Regulation 4 to a person from whom advice is sought shall be construed as a reference to the old authority.

The Act does not contain any specific provisions relating to the children of parents who are engaged in the armed forces. Such children frequently move, with their parents, from one area to another. In Paragraph 71 of the DES circular 1/83 the Secretary of State 'Requests that', where assessment procedures are initiated in relation to children whose parents are serving in the armed forces, the local education authorities, (after first obtaining the consent of the child's parent), notify the 'Service Children's Education Authority' (SCEA). The circular recommends that where a statement has been prepared, this should also be sent to the 'Service Children's Education Authority'.

The Review and Amendment of Statements

Local education authorities are under a duty to keep statements under review. The review must involve the making of an assessment of the child's special educational needs in accordance with Section 5 of the Act. In any event, a statement must be reviewed by the local education authority within the period of 12 months beginning with the making of the statement or, as the case may be, with the previous review. Such review should also involve an assessment of the child's special educational needs within the terms of Section 5 (see page 36).

If a local education authority wishes to cease to maintain or amend a statement it must not do so without first complying with the provisions of part 2 of the first schedule to the Education Act 1981. The schedule requires that a local education authority wishing to amend or to cease to maintain a statement must, before doing so, serve[10] on the parent of the child, notice in writing of its intention. The notice must inform the parent of his right to make representations.

Any parent upon whom any such notice has been served may, within the period of 15 days beginning with the date on which the notice was served, make representations to the authority about their proposals. The local education authority must consider such representations and communicate their decision to the parent in writing. These provisions relating to the amendment and maintenance of statements do not apply where a local education authority cease to maintain a statement in relation to a child who has ceased to be its responsibility or where amendments are made to a statement consequential upon the making, amendment, or revocation of a school attendance order.[11]

The Act does not contain any specific provisions relating to the right of appeal against the decision of a local education authority to amend or to cease to maintain a statement. However, it may be possible to appeal such a decision under Section 8 of the Act. The basis upon which such an appeal may be pursued is discussed in Chapter 11 (see page 89).

The Transitional Provisions

The transitional provisions which are to be found in the Second Schedule to the Education Act 1981 apply in relation to any child for whom immediately before the commencement of Section 7 of the Act a local education authority was providing special educational treatment under the Education Act 1944. As we have seen Section 8(2)(c) of the Education Act 1944 defines special educational treatment as education by special methods appropriate for persons suffering from a disability of mind or body. In the 'Handicapped Pupils and Special Schools Regulations' 1959[12], the Secretary of State defined 10 categories of disability namely, blind, partially sighted, deaf, partial hearing, delicate, educationally sub-normal, epileptic, maladjusted, physically handicapped and those suffering from speech defects. These categories include those children who were categorised in the Education (Handicapped Children) Act 1970 as severely sub-normal children.

Such children, namely those who previously required special educational treatment, are to be taken as having special educational needs. The authority shall be taken to have made an assessment of the child's educational needs and to have formed the opinion that his special educational needs call for the authority to determine the special educational provision that should be made for him. The duty to statement imposed by Section 7 of the Act is suspended for a period of 12 months and so will not come into effect until 1 April 1984. Until such time as the child is statemented the local education authority remains under a duty to continue to provide the special educational treatment which the child was receiving immediately before the commencement of Section 7 unless the child's parent makes suitable arrangements. The schedule provides that the transitional provisions are not intended to require a local education authority to behave in a way which is in any respect incompatible with a school attendance order in force under Section 37 of the 1944 Education Act.[13]

Section 8 of the Education Act 1981 is suspended until 1 April 1984 unless —

(a) The special educational provision specified in the statement, when this has been made, differs from the special educational treatment which the child was receiving before the commencement of this schedule.
(Otherwise than to take account of a School Attendance Order);
or

(b) An assesment of the child's educational needs has been made under Section 5 of the Education Act 1981 following the making of the statement.

Notes

1. For the meaning of service see page 41. For the meaning of parent see page 47 and the Table of Definitions.

2. The statutory right of appeal against a statement is discussed in Chapter 11.

3. Section 7(4)(b) of the Act.

4. Section 7(5) of the Act.

5. For the meaning of service see page 41.

6. As to those provisions see Chapter 11.

7. Although the word 'prescribed' is not defined in the Education Act 1981, the Act is to be construed as one with the Education Act 1944 which provides that 'prescribed' means prescribed by Regulations made by the Secretary of State.

8. The Regulations provide that reference to 'representations made, or evidence submitted' by a child's parent, is a reference to representations made or written evidence submitted in pursuance of Section 5(3)(d) of the Act (see Chapter 3) except that where such representations have been made orally, any reference thereto is a reference to a written summary of those representations which the parent has accepted as accurate.

9. As to the meaning of service see page 41.

10. As to the meaning of service see page 41.

11. As to the making, amendment and revocation of school attendance orders see Chapter 10.

12. S.I. 1959 No: 365.

13. As to the provisions relating to School Attendance Orders see Chapter 10.

5 THE ROLE OF HEALTH AUTHORITIES

Because of the definition of 'special educational provision' in Section 1 of the Education Act 1981 it is clear that local education authorities are empowered to make provision for children who are not old enough to attend school.

Section 10 of the Act confers a special duty in relation to children under 5 years of age. Where the area or district health authority[1] forms the opinion that the child has, or probably has, special educational needs they must bring this to the attention of the appropriate local education authority. The health authority must inform the parent of its opinion and grant the parent an opportunity to discuss this opinion prior to referring the case to the local education authority. If the health authority are of the opinion that a particular voluntary organisation is likely to be able to give the parent advice or assistance in connection with any special educational needs that the child may have they shall inform the parent accordingly.

Section 10 refers to the 'appropriate local education authority'. Presumably, this means the local education authority in whose area the child lives.

Note

1. The section anticipates the pending reorganisation of the National Health Service under Section 1 of the Health Services Act 1980 on the basis of district authorities.

6 EDUCATING CHILDREN OTHER THAN IN SCHOOLS

Section 56 of the Education Act 1944, as amended by the Education (Miscellaneous Provisions) Act 1948, provides for the education of children other than in schools in 'extraordinary circumstances':

> If a local education authority are satisfied that by reason of any extraordinary circumstance a child or young person is unable to attend a suitable school for the purpose of receiving primary or secondary education, they shall have power with the approval of the minister to make special arrangements for him to receive education otherwise than at school, being primary or secondary education, as the case may require, or, if the authority are satisfied that it is impracticable for him to receive full time education and the minister approves, education similar in other respects but less than full-time.

In the past, provision has been made for handicapped children by way of tuition both at home and in hospital.

Section 3 of the Education Act 1981 extends the power to educate children with special educational needs other than in schools by providing that:

> If, in relation to any child in their area who has special educational needs, a local education authority are satisfied that it would be inappropriate for the special educational provision required for that child, or for any part of that provision, to be made in a school, they may after consulting the child's parent arrange for it, or, as the case may be, for that part of it, to be made otherwise than in a school.

It follows therefore that the local education authority must satisfy itself that it would be 'inappropriate' for the special educational provision required by the child to be made in a school.

Consequently, the decision is one in which the local education authority have a wide discretion.

7 SPECIAL SCHOOLS AND APPROVED INDEPENDENT SCHOOLS

General

The Warnock Committee did not advocate the abolition of special schools but maintained that they should be used to educate the small minority of children with severe disabilities. Accordingly, Sections 11–14 of the Education Act 1981 make specific provision in relation to both special schools and approved independent schools.

Section 11(1) of the Education Act 1981 repeals Section 9(5) of the Education Act 1944. By Section 9(5) of the Education Act 1944 special schools were defined as 'schools which are specially organised for the purpose of providing special educational treatment for pupils requiring such treatment and are approved by the minister for that purpose'. This definition is replaced by one which refers to special educational provision rather than special educational treatment. Consequently, Section 9(5) is replaced by a new section in these terms:

> Schools which are especially organised to make special educational provision for pupils with special educational needs and which are for the time being approved by the Secretary of State as special schools shall be known as special schools.

This definition of a 'special school' applies to both maintained and non-maintained schools. Such a school must comply with the standards laid down in the Handicapped Pupils and Special Schools Regulations 1959.[1] In general, these require that the premises, organisation, admission requirements and teaching sessions meet certain specified standards. The Regulations contain additional requirements relating solely to non-maintained special schools. They require, inter alia, that such schools have a body of managers independent of the staff, and that no member of staff has a financial interest in the school.

A special school, whether it be maintained or non-maintained, must be 'approved' by the Secretary of State. The 1981 Education Act contains specific provisions relating to the granting of approval and these are discussed below. In addition to these specific provisions the second schedule to the Education Act 1981 makes transitional provision in relation to the granting of approval. It provides that where prior to the commencement of the Act the minister had given approval to a special school under Section 9(5) of the Education Act 1944, and where such approval was in force immediately before the commencement of the Education Act 1981, the approval is to have effect for the purpose of the Education Act 1944 and of the regulations made under Section 12 of the Education Act 1981 as if had been given under Section 9(5) as amended by the Education Act 1981.

Approval of Independent Schools

The provisions relating to the approval of independent schools are found in Section 11 of the Act. A local education authority may make arrangements for the provision of education for a statemented child at an independent school if one of two conditions are satisfied. The conditions are that either the school must be one which is approved by the Secretary of State as suitable for the admission of children for whom statements are maintained, or the Secretary of State must consent to the child being educated there.

By reason of Section 13 of the Education Act 1981 the Secretary of State may in relation to non-maintained schools, by regulations make provision as to:

(a) The requirements to be complied with by any school as a condition of approval of the school for the purpose of Section 11(3)(a);

(b) The requirements which are to be complied with by any school while such an approval is in force with respect to it; and

(c) The withdrawal of approval from any schools:
   (i) At the request of the proprietor;[2] or
   (ii) On the ground that there has been a failure to comply with any prescribed requirement.

Further, the Secretary of State has power to grant conditional approval. In deciding whether or not to consent to a child being educated at an independent school, the Secretary of State may impose such conditions as he sees fit.[3]

Approval of Special Schools

Section 12(1) of the Education Act 1981 provides that the Secretary of State may by regulations make provision as to:

(a) The requirements which are to be complied with by any school as a special school under Section 9(5) of the principle Act;

(b) The requirements which are to be complied with by a special school while such an approval is in force with respect to it; and

(c) The withdrawal of approval from any school —
  (i) At the request of the proprietor; or
  (ii) On the ground that there has been a failure to comply with any prescribed requirement.

Section 12(2) further provides:

Without prejudice to the generality of subsection (i) above regulations under that subsection may impose requirements, which call for arrangements to be approved by the Secretary of State.

Whilst the provisions of the Education Act 1944 directing that primary and secondary education are provided in separate schools do not apply to special schools, the Secretary of State is empowered to regulate the organisation of any special school as a primary school or as a secondary school. By Section 12(4) of the Education Act 1981 the Secretary of State must make regulations to secure that, as far as it is practical, pupils attending special schools also attend religious worship and receive religious instruction. The regulations should make provision for religious worship or instruction in accordance with the wishes of the child's parent or permit the withdrawal from religious worship or instruction of any child by his parent in accordance with the parents' wishes.

Removal of a Child from a Special School

Section 38 of the Education Act 1944, now repealed by the Education Act 1981, provided that a child could not be withdrawn from a special school without the consent of the relevant local education authority. The parent of such a child who was aggrieved by a refusal of the authority to comply with a request for consent to withdraw his child could refer the question to the minister. The minister had power to give such directions as he saw fit. Section 38(3) provided that no direction given by the minister should require a pupil to be a registered pupil at a special school without either:

(i)   the parents' consent; or
(ii) there having been issued by a medical officer of the local education authority a certificate showing that the child was suffering from some disability of mind or body of such a nature and extent that, in the opinion of the minister, it was expedient that he should attend a special school.

The removal of a child from a special school is now governed by Section 11(2) of the Education Act 1981. Section 11(2) is concerned with children of compulsory school age. Section 11(2) provides that a parent shall not withdraw his child from a special school without the consent of the local education authority. This applies to both maintained and non-maintained schools. A parent wishing to appeal a local authority's decision to retain his child in a special school may refer the matter to the Secretary of State who may direct as he thinks fit. A parent who remains dissatisfied may, in certain circumstances (see page 95), challenge the decision by way of judicial review. Since the local education authority will be under a duty to maintain a statement under Section 7 in respect of any child who is at a special school it may be open to a parent who is dissatisfied with the particular school at which his child is being educated to challenge the decision of the local education authority by adopting the appeals procedures available to a parent who wishes to challenge the contents of a statement (see Chapter 11).

Discontinuance of Maintained Special Schools

Before closing a maintained special school, the local education authority must obtain the consent of the Secretary of State. Parents of pupils and prospective pupils have a right to be informed or notified of the proposed closure. Such notice should indicate when the planned closures are to occur and specify a period, not less than 2 months, during which written objections may be made. The local education authority must submit all written objections to the Secretary of State within one month of the specified period for making objections. The Secretary of State must then accept or reject the proposals. He cannot vary the proposals. If he accepts the proposals there is no duty on the local education authority to implement them.

Notes

1. S.I. 1959 No. 365.
2. Proprietor is defined in Section 114 of the Education Act 1944 as, in relation to any school, the person or body of persons responsible for the management of the school, and in relation to applications for the registration of independent schools, includes any person or body of persons proposing to be so responsible.
3. Paragraph 30 of DES circular 8/81 states that conditions of approval will usually relate to such matters as arrangements for the involvement of parents.

8   CHILDREN IN CARE

The Act does not contain any specific provisions relating to children with special educational needs who are in care. However, the 1981 Act is to be read as one with the 1944 Act, Section 114 of which provides that 'parent' includes a guardian or any person who has the actual custody of the child or young person.[1] The DES circular 1/83 states that where a child is in care, it will be for the Director of Social Services to involve the child's natural parent according to the circumstances of each case.

By Section 87 of the Children Act 1975 a person has 'actual custody' of a child if he or she has 'actual possession of his person, whether or not that possession is shared with one or more persons'. It is submitted therefore that parents of children in care, whose children live with them, should be regarded as a 'parent' for the purposes of the Education Act 1981 and consequently should where appropriate be fully involved in the assessment process.

Where children are placed with foster parents, the foster parents clearly have 'actual custody' and should be regarded as a 'parent' within the terms of the Act. Where children are in residential care the 'person appointed to adopt the parental role' will be similarly involved.

The Child Care Act 1980 provides that in reaching any decision in relation to a child in their care local authorities[2] must give 'first consideration to the need to safeguard and promote the welfare of the child throughout his childhood and shall so far as is practicable ascertain the wishes and the feelings of the child regarding the decision and give due consideration to them, having regard to his age and understanding'. It is submitted that this provision applies to decisions taken by local authorities in relation to the Education Act 1981.

Notes

1. See table of definitions and terms for the meaning of 'parent'.

2. Local authority is defined by Section 87 of the Child Care Act as the council, of a county (other than a metropolitan county), of a metropolitan district or of a London borough or the Common Council of the City of London.

9   PARENTAL CHOICE OF SCHOOL

The General Duty

The general duty upon a local education authority to consider the wishes of parents is contained in Section 76 of the Education Act 1944, which provides that:

> In the exercise and performance of all powers and duties conferred and imposed on them by this Act the Minister and local education authorities shall have regard to the general principle that, so far as is compatible with the provision of efficient instruction and training and the avoidance of unreasonable public expenditure, pupils are to be educated in accordance with the wishes of their parents.

Section 76 was considered by the Court of Appeal in *CUMMINGS and OTHERS -v- BIRKENHEAD CORPORATION* (1971) 2 WLR 1458. In this case the Birkenhead Education Committee distributed a circular to the parents of children attending primary schools. The circular stated that of the children who were about to begin their secondary education, those who had previously been educated in Catholic schools would be considered only for Catholic secondary schools, and those who had previously been attending non-Catholic primary schools would be considered only for non-Catholic secondary schools. The parents were sent a form and invited to select a school from one of the two groups, either Catholic or non-Catholic, depending upon the type of primary school the child had attended. The Plaintiffs argued that the authority were in breach of Section 76 in that the authority were disregarding the wishes of parents. In his judgment Lord Denning M.R. referred to the earlier case of *WATT -v- KESTEVEN COUNTY COUNCIL* (1955) 1 Q.B. 408 and commented:

> We then pointed out that the wishes of the parents are only one thing. There are many other things to which the education

authority may have regard and which may outweigh the wishes of the parents. They must have regard, for instance, not only to the wishes of the parents of one particular child, but also to the wishes of the parents of other children and of other groups of children.

It follows therefore that the wishes of the parent are not the sole or overriding consideration, but one factor has to be considered.

How to Express a Choice

The parent of a child with special educational needs in respect of whom the local education authority maintain a statement should make his views known to the authority during the assessment procedures (see Chapter 3). If necessary the parent may exercise his statutory right of appeal (see Chapter 11). There may however be instances where the parent of a child considers that his child has special educational needs, but where the local education authority consider that the child's needs are not such as to require that they maintain a statement in respect of the child. In such circumstances the parent may exercise his right of appeal to the Secretary of State. If the Secretary of State refuses to direct the local education authority to reconsider their decision, of if the authority maintains its decision after reconsideration, there is no further right of appeal under the Education Act 1981.

Despite having exhausted his right of appeal under the Education Act 1981 the parent of a child who considers that his child has special educational needs, but who the local education authority do not treat as such, may be able to 'express a preference' as to which school his child attends, and if his preference is not adopted, lodge a 'School choice appeal' under the Education Act 1980. For this reason the provisions of the Education Act 1980 are discussed in this chapter despite the provision of Section 4 of the Education Act 1980 (as amended by the third schedule to the Education Act 1981) which provides that, none of the provisions of Section 6, 7 and 8 (the provision relating to school choice appeals) other than subsections (5) and (7) of the Education Act 1980 shall have effect 'in relation to special schools or children in respect of whom statements are maintained under Section 7 of the Education Act

1981 (Special education needs)'.
Section 6(1) of the Education Act 1980 provides that:

Every local education authority shall make arrangements for enabling the parent of a child in the area of the authority to express a preference as to the school at which he wishes education to be provided for his child in the exercise of the authority's functions and to give reasons for his preference.

Save in certain excepted circumstances it is the duty of the local education authority, and of the governors of a county or voluntary school concerned, to comply with any preference expressed in accordance with the arrangements (Section 6(2) of the Education Act 1980). The excepted circumstances are:

(a) if compliance with the preference would prejudice the provision of efficient education, or the efficient use of resources;

(b) if the preferred school is an aided or special agreement school and compliance with the preference would be incompatible with any arrangements between the governors and the local education authority in respect of the admission of pupils to the school; or

(c) if the arrangements for admission to the preferred school are based wholly or partly on a selection by reference to ability or aptitude and compliance with the preference would be incompatible with selection under the arrangements.
(Section 6(3) of the Education Act 1980).

The duty imposed by Section 6 is an absolute one and, subject to the excepted circumstances, a local education authority does not have a discretion as to whether or not to comply with the parents' wishes. One important consequence of the section is that it enables the parent of a child in respect of whom the local education authority do not maintain a statement to express a preference for a school best equipped to cater for his child's particular needs.

To enable parents to decide which schools are most suitable for their children Section 8 of the Education Act 1980 requires local education authorities and governors to furnish information for parents including information about the criteria for school admission, the 'arrangements' which have been made pursuant to Section 6 of the Education Act 1980 for parents to express a preference as to a particular school, and the numbers to be admitted to the school in the age group concerned. For the precise nature of the information which local education authorities and governors must make available, reference should be made both to Section 8 of the Education Act 1980 and to the Education (School Information) Regulations 1981. The Education (School Information) Regulations 1981 stipulate the minimum information which local education authorities must provide in respect of both ordinary and special schools.

The duty to comply with a parent's preference imposed by Section 6 applies to any application for admission to a school maintained by a local education authority, whether or not the child is in the area of that authority. However, the duty to make arrangements for the expression of preferences only applies to the parents of children in the authority's area.

The duty also extends to applications under Section 10(3) and 11(1) of the Education Act 1980 (see pages 83–85).

Section 6 of the Education Act 1980 refers to 'preference' and not 'preferences' and it is submitted that it is implicit in this that the statutory duty imposed by this Section only applies to the first preference. The position where 2 parents living separately both express preferences is unclear, since the section refers to the 'parent', and not 'parents'. It appears that the local education authority have a discretion as to which preference they treat as a preference made under Section 6 of the Education Act 1980.

School Choice Appeal under the Education Act 1980

By Section 7 of the Education Act 1980 local education authorities must make arrangements by which parents may appeal against a decision made by, or on behalf of, a local education authority as to the school at which a child is to be educated; and against any decision made by or on behalf of the governors of a county or controlled school maintained by the authority refusing the child admission to such a school. The governors of every aided or special agreement school must also make similar arrangements for enabling the parent of a child to appeal against any decision made by or on behalf of the governors refusing the child admission to the school.

Appeals under Section 7 are known as school choice appeals. An appeal is to a committee constituted in accordance with Part 2 of Schedule 2 to the Education Act 1980. This machinery has been adopted for the purposes of appeals against statements under the Education Act 1981 and the constitution of the appeals committees together with procedures applicable to such appeals are discussed in detail in Chapter 11.[1] In relation to appeals under the Education Act 1980, the decision of the appeal committee will be binding on the local education authority or governors by or on whose behalf the decision under appeal was made, and, in the case of a decision made by, or on behalf of a local education authority, on the governors of any county or controlled school at which the committee determines that a place should be offered to the child in question. The position is different in the case of appeals under the 1981 Act. The nature and reasons for the distinction between appeals under the 1980 and 1981 Act is discussed in Chapter 11. It is significant, however, that whilst after an appeal under Section 8 of the Education Act 1981 a parent who remains dissatisfied may appeal to the Secretary of State, no such option is open to a dissatisfied appellant under Section 7 of the Education Act 1980.

It should be remembered that a parent may refer a case to the Secretary of State if he feels that the local education authority or the governors of the school have behaved unreasonably or that they have failed to discharge a duty imposed upon them. These general powers are discussed on page 93.

Notes

1. The Association of Metropolitan Authorities, in consultation with the Council on Tribunals (see page 92) have issued a Code of Practice for school choice appeals. This is included in the appendices to this book.

10 SCHOOL ATTENDANCE ORDERS

General

Section 36 of the Education Act 1944, as amended by Section 17 of the Education Act 1981, provides that it is the duty of the parent of every child of compulsory school age[1] to cause him to receive efficient full-time education suitable to his age, ability and aptitude and to any special educational needs he may have either by regular attendance at school or otherwise. Section 37 of the Education Act 1944 was designed to ensure that parents fulfilled this duty. Section 37(1) which remains in force as amended by the Education Act 1981 provides that:

If it appears to a local education authority that the parent of any child of compulsory school age in their area is failing to perform the duty imposed on him by the last foregoing section, it shall be the duty of the authority to serve upon the parent a notice requiring him within such time as may be specified in the notice, being not less than 14 days, from the service thereof, to satisfy the authority that the child is receiving efficient full-time education suitable to his age, ability and aptitude and to any special educational needs he may have either by regular attendance at school or otherwise.

Subsection (2) of Section 37 as amended by Section 21 of the Education Act 1981 further provides that:

If, after such a notice has been served upon a parent by a local education authority, the parent fails to satisfy the authority in accordance with the requirements of the notice that the child to whom the notice relates is receiving efficient full-time education suitable to his age, ability and aptitude, then, if in the opinion of the authority it is expedient that he should attend school, the authority shall serve upon the parent an order in the prescribed form (hereafter referred to as the 'School Attendance Order')

79

requiring him to cause the child to become a registered pupil at a school named in the order.

Section 37 is supplemented by Section 15 of the Education Act 1981. Section 15 applies where the local education authority propose to serve a school attendance order on the parent of a state-mented child.[2] It does not apply to children in respect of whom the local education authority do not maintain a statement. Section 15 provides that the attendance order shall not be served until the expiry of 15 days beginning with the day upon which the local education authority serve upon the parent a written notice. The written notice must notify the parent of the intention of the local education authority to serve an order and it must state that if, before the expiry of that period, the parent selects a school at which he desires his child to become a registered pupil, that school will, unless the Secretary of State otherwise directs, be named in the order.

The attendance order should not be served on the parent until a period 15 days, beginning with the date on which the authority served the notice, has elapsed. It is submitted that the notice required by Section 15(2) of the Education Act 1981 is in addition to that required under Section 37 of the Education Act 1944. The respective periods of notice required by the two sections differ, and the notice specified in Section 15 does not require the parent to show that the child is receiving efficient full-time education suitable to his age, ability and aptitude.

If before the expiry of the period specified in the notice required by Section 15(2) the parent selects a school to be named in the order, that school (unless the Secretary of State otherwise directs) must be named in the order. However, the local education authority may apply to the Secretary of State for a direction determining what school is to be named in the order. Section 15(4) specifies the circumstances in which such an application may be made. The local education authority must be of the opinion that:

(a) the school selected by the parent as the school to be named in the order is unsuitable to the child's age, his ability or aptitude or to his special educational needs; or

(b) that the attendance of the child at the school so selected would prejudice the provision of efficient education or the efficient use of resources.

Before making such an application to the Secretary of State, the local education authority must give the child's parent notice of their intention to apply to the Secretary of State for a determination. The reference in Section 15(4)(b) to 'efficient education' presumably means the efficient education of all children and not simply the child concerned.

Amendment and Revocation: Statemented Children

The following provisions which relate to the amendment and revocation of school attendance orders apply in any case where,

(a) A local education authority has served a school attendance order on the parent of a child under Section 37 of the Education Act 1944 (i); and

(b) The local education authority maintains a statement in relation to a child (see page 49).

After an attendance order has been made in respect of a statemented child a dissatisfied parent may make an application to the local education authority that another school be substituted for that named in the order, or, he may apply to the local education authority that the existing order be revoked on the ground that arrangements have been made for his child to receive efficient full-time education suitable to his age, ability and aptitude and to his special educational needs otherwise than at school. The local education authority must grant such a request unless they are of the opinion that:

(i)   the school selected by the parent as the school to be named in the order is unsuitable to the child's age, ability or aptitude or to his special educational needs, or that the proposed change of school is against the interest of the child: or

(ii) the attendance of the child at the school so selected would prejudice the provision of efficient education or the efficient use of resources; or

(iii) no satisfactory arrangement has been made for the education of the child otherwise that at school, (Section 16(2) of the Education Act 1981).

Appeals Against the Refusal to Vary or Revoke a School Attendance Order: Statemented Children

A parent who is aggrieved by the refusal of a local education authority to revoke or amend a school attendance order may refer the case to the Secretary of State (Section 16(3) of the Education Act 1981). The Secretary of State must make such directions as he thinks fit. He may require the local education authority to amend the statement if that is 'necessary or expedient' (Section 16(4) of the Education Act 1981). If the Secretary of State directs that a different school be substituted for that named in the school attendance order it is the duty of the local education authority and of the governors of that school to admit the child to the school (Section 16(5) of the Education Act 1981).

It should be appreciated that local education authorities remain under the general duty under Section 2 of the Education Act 1981 to arrange the special educational provision for statemented children in ordinary schools. Accordingly, disputes may arise where parents insist that local education authorities are in breach of Section 2 of the Act because the school named in the attendance order is not an ordinary school.

Transitional Provisions

We have seen that Sections 15 and 16 apply in relation to statemented children. Prior to such a statement being made under the transitional provisions Section 15 and Section 16 will apply, save that the requirement that the authority 'maintain a statement' for the child under Section 7 is replaced by the requirement that the local education authority were 'immediately before the commencement of Section 7, providing special educational treatment for that child under the Education Act 1944'.

Attendance Orders: Non-Statemented Children

It is clear that because of the wide definition of special educational need in the Education Act 1981 and the wide discretion that authorities have as to whether or not to prepare a statement in relation to a child, there may be children with special educational needs in respect of whom local education authorities do not maintain statements (see pages 49–51). Such children do not fall within the provisions of Section 15 of the Education Act 1981. They may, however, fall within the ambit of Section 10[3] of the Education Act 1980 which makes similar provisions in relation to such children as that made in relation to statemented children by Section 15 of the Education Act 1981. Section 10(1)–(4) of the Education Act 1980 provides:

(1) Before serving a school attendance order on a parent under Section 37 of the Education Act 1944 the local education authority shall serve on him a written notice of their intention to serve the order —

(a) specifiying the school which they intend to name in the order and, if they think fit, one or more other schools which they regard as suitable alternatives; and

(b) stating the effect of subsections (2) to (4) below:

but no aided or special agreement school shall be specified in the notice without the consent of the school.

(2) If the notice specifies one or more alternative schools and the parent selects one of them before the expiration of the period of fourteen days beginning with the day after that on which the notice is served, the school selected by him shall be named in the order.

(3) If before the expiration of that period the parent —

(a) applies for the child to be admitted to a school maintained by a local education authority and, if that authority is not the one by whom the notice was served, notifies the latter authority of the application; or

(b) applies to the local education authority by whom the notice was served for education to be provided for the child at a school not maintained by a local education authority,

then, if the child is offered a place at a school as a result of the application mentioned in paragraph (a) above or is offered a place at a school at which the local education authority agree to provide education for him in response to the application mentioned in paragraph (b) above, that school shall be named in the order.

(4) If before the expiration of the period mentioned in sub-section (2) above the parent —

(a) applies for the child to be admitted to a school which is not maintained by a local education authority and in respect of which makes no such application as is mentioned in subsection (3)(b) above; and

(b) notifies the local education authority by whom the notice was served of the application,

then, if as a result of the application the child is offered a place at a school which is suitable to his age, ability and aptitude, that school shall be named in the order.

The effect of these provisions may be summarised as follows. The local education authority may serve[4] upon a parent a notice requiring the parent to satisfy the authority that his child is receiving efficient full-time education. The authority may name any school or schools in the notice, save that the school so named must not be an aided or special agreement school (except where the governors consent). The parent may then pursue one of three courses —

(a) accept one of the schools so named, or

(b) apply for the admission of the child to another maintained school or non-maintained school; (within 14 days) or,

(c) apply himself to a non-maintained school for the child to be admitted (within 14 days).

If the parent follows course 'a', that school will be named in the order. If the child is offered a place in consequence of the parent following course 'b', that school will be named in the order. If the parent follows course 'b', in respect of a non-maintained school to be provided by the local education authority, this request must be considered under Section 6(5)(b) of the Education Act 1980. Conse-quently the duty of the authority to comply with such a request applies in the same way as it does to a parent's, 'school preference' made under Section 6(1) of the Education Act 1980 (see page 75ff.). It follows that the 'exceptions in Section 6(3) of the Education Act 1980 will apply to such applications' (see page 75). If the parent follows course 'b' the parent must, within 14 days, seek admission to the school preferred. The school may be a school outside the area of the local education authority responsible for serving the order. The parent must of course comply with the local rules for expressing a preference which have been established by the authority pursuant to the duty imposed by Section 6 of the Education Act 1980. If admission is refused, the parent may lodge a school choice appeal under Section 7 of the Education Act 1980 (see page 76ff.). The local education authority should stay further action until the outcome of such an appeal is known. If the appeal is unsuccessful the authority may name in the order the school, or one of the schools, originally proposed.

If the parents follows course 'c', the school shall be named in the order, if it is suitable to the age, ability and aptitude of the child.

In contrast with Section 15 of the Education Act 1981,[6] there is no provision in Section 10 of the Education Act 1980 for the local education authority to apply to the Secretary of State for a direction determining what school is to be named in an order.

Amendment and Revocation of Attendance Orders: Non-Statemented Children

The relevant section is Section 11 of the Education Act 1980 which provides that:

(1) If at any time while a school attendance order is in force with respect to a child the parent —
   (a) applies for the child to be admitted to a school maintained by a local education authority; or
   (b) applies to the local education authority by whom the order was served for education to be provided for the child at a school not maintained by a local education authority,
   being, in either case, a school different from the one named in the order, then, if the child is offered a place at a school as a result of the application mentioned in paragraph (a) above or is offered a place at a school at which the local education authority agree to provide education for him in response to the application mentioned in paragraph (b) above, the local authority by whom the order was served shall at the request of the parent amend the order by substituting that school

for the one previously named.
(2) If at any time while a school attendance order is in force with respect to a child —
  (a) the parent applies for the child to be admitted to a school which is not maintained by a local education authority and in respect of which he makes no such application as is mentioned in subsection (1)(b) above, being a school different from the one named in the order; and
  (b) as a result of the application the child is offered a place at a school which is suitable to his age, ability and aptitude, [and to any special educational needs he may have][5]

the local education authority by whom the order was served shall at the request of the parent amend the order by substituting that school for one previously named.

The effect of Section 11 is that a parent may seek to amend an attendance order in one of 3 ways.

1. He may apply for his child's admission to a maintained school other than the one named in the order. Such an application should be considered under Section 6(5)(b) of the Education Act 1980 and accordingly, in the context of the local education authority's and school governors' duty to comply with the parent's preference.[7]

2. He may apply that the authority provide a place at a non-maintained school.[8]
   The application must be considered in accordance with Section 6(5)(b) of the Education Act 1980. (Section 6(5)(b) provides that Section 6(2) of the Education Act 1980 applies to applications under Section 11(1) of the Education Act 1980.)
   If the child is offered a place at the school for which application is made, the order must be amended.

3. He may himself apply directly for a place at a non-maintained school. In this case the school must be named in the order only if the school is suitable to the age, aptitude, ability and special educational needs of the child concerned. The duty imposed by Section 6(2) of the Education Act 1980[9] does not apply where the parent makes a direct application for a place at a non-maintained school.

The provisions relating to the revocation of school attendance orders made in respect of non-statemented children are to be found in Section 37(4) of the Education Act 1944. Such an order may be revoked if the child is receiving efficient and suitable full-time education other than at school. A parent who is dissatisfied with a refusal to revoke an order may appeal to the Secretary of State.

Notes

1. See table of definition and terms.
2. Similar 'additional provisions' are made in respect of non-statemented children by Section 10 of the Education Act 1980, see page 83.
3. Section 10 came into force on 1 July 1982.
4. See page 41 for the meaning of Service.
5. The words in square brackets were inserted by the Education Act 1981 Section 21, Schedule 3.
6. See page 80.
7. See page 75. Section 6(5)(b) provides that Section 6(2) of the Education Act 1980 applies to applications under Section 11(1) of the Education Act 1980.
8. By reason of Section 9 of the Education Act 1944 and the Education (Miscellaneous Provisions) Act 1953 a local education authority has power to provide education in a non-maintained school. Section 28 of the Education Act 1980 abolishes the requirement that the authority should first obtain consent from the Secretary of State. The requirement continues to apply in relation to statemented children.
9. See page 75.

11 APPEALS

The Appeals which are available to an aggrieved parent wishing to challenge the decision of a local education authority in relation to his child's special educational needs may be to:

(i)   a local Appeal Committee;
(ii) the Secretary of State;
(iii) the courts, by way of an application for judicial review.

This chapter is intended to be an outline of the circumstances in which these procedures are available.

Appeals to the Local Appeal Committee

The Availability of an Appeal to the Local Appeal Committee

Section 8(1) of the Education Act 1981 provides that:

> Every Local Education Authority shall make arrangements for enabling the parent of a child in respect of whom they maintain a statement under Section 7 to appeal, following the first or any subsequent assessment of the child's educational needs under Section 5, against the special educational provision specified in this statement.

Such an appeal is to a local appeal committee.

If the child concerned is not a child in respect of whom the local education authority maintain a statement there will be no appeal to the local appeal committee under the Education Act 1981. However, the local appeal committees were set up under the Education Act 1980 and the parent of a non-statemented child may have a right to appeal to a local appeal committee under that statute. By Section 7 of the Education Act 1980 such an appeal will lie against:

(i) any decision made by or on behalf of the Authority as to the school at which education is to be provided for a child in the exercise of the local education authority's function, and

(ii) any decision made by, or on behalf of governors of a county or controlled school maintained by the local education authority refusing the child admission to such a school.

The Education Act 1980 provides that the decision of the appeal committee on any appeal shall be binding upon the local education authority or governors by or on whose behalf the decision under appeal was made and, in the case of a decision made by or on behalf of a local education authority, on the governors of any county or controlled school in which the Committee determines that a place should be offered to the child in question. Section 7 of the Education Act 1980 does not apply to special schools, nursery schools or to children under 5 years of age.[1]

In the DES circular 8/81 a distinction is drawn between the respective functions of the local appeals committees under the Education Act 1980 and the Education Act 1981:

When hearing appeals under the 1980 Act an appeal committee will normally be faced with relatively simple school admission issues, the assumption being essentially that, unless a selective system is in operation, ordinary schools are suitable for all children in their age group. This is not the case in a dispute over special educational provision. Location will often be influenced not only by availability of schools staffed and equipped to cater for particular handicaps but also by the availability of, for instance, health or social services and any of these may be determining factors as to the appropriate setting in which special educational needs are catered for. It is therefore likely that disputes between parents and local education authorities will sometimes involve an appeal committee in examining a very wide variety of specialist advice, given the range of complex handicapping conditions from which children can suffer. The issue will differ greatly from the normal run of schools admission cases. For this reason, after hearing an appeal from the parents of a child for whom a statement of special needs is maintained, an appeal committee will not be able to overrule a local education authority if they disagree with their proposals. Instead they have the power to refer the case back to the local education authority with their observations.

The Constitution of the Local Appeals Committees and the Procedure for Making an Appeal

The appeal committee must be constituted in accordance with Paragraph 1 of Part 1 of Schedule 2 to the Education Act 1980. The appeal committee will consist of three, five or seven members nominated by the local education authority from among persons appointed by the authority under the Schedule. The appeal committee members may be drawn from two groups, those who are members of the local education authority, or of any education committee of the authority and those who are not members of the local education authority or of any education committee of the authority but who are experienced in education and are acquainted with the educational conditions in the area of the authority, or are parents of registered pupils at the school. The appointed appeal committee members shall not include anyone employed by the local education authority otherwise than as a teacher. The appeal committee members who fall into the first group shall not outnumber those falling within the second category by more than one. Further, a person who is a member of an education committee of the authority shall not be the chairman of the appeal committee. A person shall not be a member of an appeal committee for the consideration of any appeal against a decision if he was amongst those who made the decision or took part in discussions as to whether the decision should be made.

If the issue is as to whether or not a child should be admitted to a particular school, no teacher at that school shall be a member of the appeal committee. Unfortunately, the 'neutrality' of the appeal committee is questionable for two reasons,

(i)   the committee members of both categories are nominated by the local education authority; and
(ii) There may be a majority on the committee of persons drawn from the first category, albeit that no person appointed as a committee member shall be a person employed by the local education authority otherwise than as a teacher.

The local appeals committees are subject to the provisions of the Tribunals and Enquiries Act 1971 which governs the composition and procedures of the tribunals to which it applies. The Tribunals and Enquiries Act 1958 (now superseded by the Tribunals and Enquiries Act 1971) established the Council on Tribunals which performs the task of supervising various tribunals including the local appeals committees. It consists of between 10 and 15 members appointed by the Lord Chancellor. The main task of the Council is to keep under review the constitution and operation of a number of tribunals and enquiries, including those of the local appeal committee. The Council has beeen in consultation with the Department of Education and the Association of Metropolitan Authorities regarding sections of the Education Act 1980 and the Education Act 1981. During 1982 a code of practice was issued and circulated to all local authorities by the Association of Metropolitan Authorities. An addendum containing guidance on appeals under the Education Act 1981 has also been approved and circulated to all local authorities. Extracts from the Code of Practice, incorporating the addendum, are included in the appendices to this book.[2]

Whilst the views of the Council on Tribunals are by no means binding upon the local appeals committees their views as to the procedures adopted by tribunals and enquiries may be persuasive and consequently a parent dissatisfied with the procedures relating to an appeal to a local appeal committee should consider referring the matter to the Council for their consideration. Part 2 of the Second Schedule to the Education Act 1980 (as modified by Section 8 of the Education Act 1981) provides for the procedure to be followed in making an appeal under Section 8 of the Education Act 1981. The Schedule provides that an appeal shall be by notice in writing setting out the grounds on which it is made. An appellant may be present at the appeal, he may make oral representations and he may be accompanied by a friend or representative. Presumably, the reference in the Schedule to an appellant being represented includes legal representation. The appeal committee must take into account in considering the appeal any representations made by the appellant under Section 7 of the Education Act 1981. The decision of the appeal committee may be a majority decision and in the event of deadlock the chairman will have a casting vote. The decision of an appeal committee, and the grounds on which the decision was made shall be communicated by the committee in writing to both the appellant and the local education authority.

Where the appeal is against the decision made by or on behalf of the governors of the county or controlled school the governors should be notified in writing of the decision.

Appeals should be heard in private except when otherwise directed by the authority but a member of the local education authority may attend as an observer. Similarly, a member of the Council on Tribunals may also attend to observe the proceedings. It is important to note that, where an appeal is made under the Education Act 1981, the decision of the appeal committee is not binding upon the local education authority.[3]

Appeals to the Secretary of State

The Secretary of State has general powers under Section 68 and Section 99 of the Education Act 1944 to review the decisions of local education authorities.[4]

By Section 68 of the Education Act 1944, the Secretary of State may, either 'upon complaint of any person or otherwise', prevent the unreasonable exercise of a power or duty by a local education authority or the governors of a school. He may exercise this power even if the duty or power is expressed in subjective language such as 'in the opinion of the local education authority'. He may give such directions as to the exercise of the power or the performance of the duty as appear to him to be expedient.

By Section 99 of the Education Act 1944, either 'upon complaint by any interested party or otherwise', the Secretary of State may, if he is satisfied that any local education authority or governors of a school have failed to discharge any duty imposed upon them by or for the purpose of the Act,[5] make an order declaring the authority or governors to be in default of that duty and give directions to enforce the execution of the duty.

In addition to these general powers, we have already seen that the Education Act 1981 contains specific provisions for an aggrieved parent, in certain instances, to appeal to the Secretary of State. Section 5(6) of the Education Act 1981 provides that a parent may appeal to the Secretary of State against a refusal by a local education authority to determine the special educational provision that should be made for his child (see page 36). Further, a parent who remains dissatisfied with the decision of a local appeal committee pursuant to an appeal under Section 8 of the Education Act 1981 may appeal in writing to the Secretary of State. Such an appeal is available where:

(a) the appeal committee confirms the decision of the local education authority as to the special educational provision to be made for the child; or

(b) the local education authority informs the appellant of their decision in a case which has been remitted to them under Section 8(4)(b) (Section 8(4)(b) refers to the situation where the local appeal committee remits the case to the local education authority for consideration in the light of the committee's observations).

Upon hearing an appeal pursuant to Section 8 and after consulting the local education authority, the Secretary of State may,

(a) confirm special educational provision specified in the statement;

(b) amend the statement so far as it specifies the special educational provision and make such other consequential amendments to the statement as he considers appropriate; or

(c) direct the local education authority to cease to maintain the statement.

It is important to appreciate that where an appeal to the Secretary of State is made, pursuant to Section 5 of the Education Act 1981 (that is, where the appeal is made against the decision of a local education authority not to determine the special educational provision that should be made for the child), the Secretary of State does not have any power to compel a local education authority to behave in a particular way, though he may direct the authority to reconsider its decision.

The parent of a statemented child may appeal to the Secretary of State against the refusal of the local education authority to vary or revoke a school attendance order (Section 16 of the Education Act 1981). For detailed discussion as to the Secretary of State's powers upon such an appeal reference should be made to page 82.

Challenging the Decision of a Local Education Authority by way of Judicial Review

We have seen that there are numerous instances under the Education Act 1981 where the local education authority, and in some instances the governors of schools, are entrusted with a statutory discretion. Such discretion implies some choice as to whether or not, and in some instances how, certain action is to be taken. These areas of discretion are usually marked by subjective language such as 'if the local education authority is satisfied that', or 'if the local education authority is of the opinion that'. Some of the more important examples in the Act are:

Section 3 — If, in relation to any child in their area who has special educational needs, a local education authority are satisfied that it would be inappropriate for the special educational provision required for that child . . . they may arrange for it . . . to be made otherwise than in a school.

Section 5(1) — Where in the case of a child for whom the local education authority are responsible, the authority are of the opinion . . . they shall make an assessment of his educational needs.

Section 5(4) — Where a local education authority have served a notice under sub-section 3 above . . . the authority shall, if they consider it appropriate . . . assess the educational needs of the child concerned.

Section 6(1) — Where, in the case of a child in their area who is under the age of 2 years, a local education authority are of the opinion . . . they may with the consent of the child's parent make an assessment.

Section 6(2) — An assessment under this Section shall be made in such manner as the local education authority consider appropriate.

Section 7(1) — Where an assessment has been made in respect of a child under Section 5 the local education authority . . . shall if they are of the opinion that they should determine the special educational provision that should be made for him, make a statement.

Section 9(1) — If a parent of a child . . . for whom no statement is maintained . . . asks the authority to arrange for an assessment to be made . . . the authority shall comply with the request unless it is in their opinion unreasonable.

Section 9(2) — If the parent of a child for whom the local education authority maintain a statement . . . asks the authority to arrange for an assessment . . . the authority shall comply with the request unless they are satisfied that an assessment would be inappropriate.

Further, there are a number of instances where the Act confers a discretion upon the Secretary of State, for example,

Section 5(8) — On an appeal under sub-section 6 above the Secretary of State may, if he thinks fit, direct the local education authority to reconsider their decision.

Section 8(7) — On an appeal under sub-section 6 above, the Secretary of State may, . . . — confirm the special educational provision specified in the statement;

(b) amend the statement. . . .

(c) direct the local education authority to cease to maintain the statement.

In addition to these examples where the Act bestows a discretion upon a particular body or individual, there are many instances where the legislation imposes a duty or confers a power to behave in a particular way.

Whenever a body or individual seeks to exercise a discretion or power, or carry out a duty conferred by statute, the courts will in certain circumstances intervene to ensure that those so acting do so in accordance with the law and in good faith. The procedure by which a parent may challenge the exercise of a discretion or power, or the performance of a duty, is by way of an application for judicial review to the High Court. If, for example, a local education authority failed to permit a parent the requisite 29 days (Section 5) in which to make representations regarding an assessment of his child, it is clear that the authority would, by so doing err in law, and in such circumstances the courts would grant relief to remedy the error.

However, as has been noted, there are many sections of the Act which confer upon local education authorities, and in some instances upon the Secretary of State, a discretion. If it is clear that there has been an error in law, or where the discretion has been exercised unreasonably or, in bad faith, those so erring or behaving unreasonably may be subject to judicial control. The concepts of 'reasonableness' and 'bad faith' tend, in practical terms to amount to the same thing and the test for 'bad faith', which is rarely regarded as a synonym for dishonesty, is often expressed in this way; is this a decision which a reasonable body of this nature could have reached? If it is, a court would not interfere with the decision. A court will not interfere merely on the basis that it would have reached a different conclusion to that reached by the body or individual concerned.

The best known exposition of the principles applied by the courts in such cases was given by Lord Green M. R. in *ASSOCIATED PROVINCIAL PICTURE HOUSES LIMITED -v- WEDNESBURY CORPORATION* (1948) 1 KB 223 in these terms:

> The exercise of such a discretion must be a real exercise of the discretion. If, in the statute conferring the discretion there is to be found expressly or by implication matters which the authority exercising the discretion ought to have regard to, then in exercising the discretion it must have regard to those matters. Conversely, if the nature of the subject matter and the general interpretation makes it clear that certain matters would not be germain to the matter in question the authority must disregard those irrelevant collateral matters . . . a person entrusted with a discretion must, so to speak, direct himself properly in law. He must course his own attention to the matters which he is bound to consider. He must exclude from his consideration matters which are irrelevant to what he has to consider. If he does not obey those rules, he may truly be said, and often is said, to be acting unreasonably. Similarly, there may be something so

absurd that no sensible person could ever dream that it lay within the powers of the authority.

The limits of legal reasonableness are often unclear, the identification of which is by no means an easy task. Within those limits lies an area in which those upon whom a statutory discretion is conferred may exercise judgment. If the limits are exceeded the decision will be open to correction in the courts.

An example of the approach adopted by the courts, is to be found in *THE SECRETARY OF STATE FOR EDUCATION AND SCIENCE -v- THAMESIDE METROPOLITAN BOROUGH COUNCIL* (1977) A.C. 1014. This was a case where after a local election the new council proceeded to reverse their predecessors scheme for introducing comprehensive schools. The Secretary of State, favouring comprehensive schools, issued a statutory direction to the new council to proceed with the original scheme. The relevant statute empowered him to issue directions if he was 'satisfied . . . that any local authority . . . have acted or were proposing to act unreasonably' in performing their statutory functions. The new council resisted his direction and the Secretary of State therefore applied for an order of mandamus to compel the council to comply. This was refused by the Court of Appeal and the decision was appealed to the House of Lords. In his judgement in the House of Lords, Lord Wilberforce explained the proper approach:

> The section is framed in a 'subjective' form — if the Secretary of State is 'satisfied'. This form of section is quite well known and at first sight might seem to exclude judicial review on what is, or what has become a matter of pure judgment. But I do not think that they go further than that. If a judgment requires, before it can be made, the exercise of some facts, then although the evaluation of those facts is for the Secretary of State alone, the court must enquire whether those facts exist, and have been taken into account, whether the judgment has been made upon a proper self-direction as to the facts, whether the judgment has not been made upon other facts which ought not to have been taken into account.

Consequently, where the Education Act 1981 confers a discretion, and specifies that particular matters are to be taken into account in the exercise of that discretion the courts will interfere if it is clear that the body or individual exercising the decretion has failed to take those matters into account, or if such a body or individual has taken other irrelevant matters into account. However, this is not to say that where the statute confers a discretion as to which matters a body or individual should take account of in reaching a decision, that the body or individual may not have regard to considerations of policy. In *CUMMING -v- BIRKENHEAD CORPORATION* (1971) 2 WR 1459 the decision of a local authority was challenged on the ground that the authority had fettered its discretion to have regard to parental wishes under Section 76 of the Education Act 1944.[6] Lord Denning M.R. applied a Test very much akin to that stated in *THE SECRETARY OF STATE FOR EDUCATION AND SCIENCE -v- TAMESIDE METROPOLITAN BOROUGH COUNCIL —*

> I desire to say at once that it is perfectly legitimate for an administrative body such as this, an education authority, to lay down a general policy which it proposes to adopt in the cases coming before it . . . One of the best-known cases is that of the married women teachers. The Education authority of Poole laid it down as their policy that 'the retention of married women teachers is inadvisable and they recommend that notice be given' to them . . . reason was that they had more than enough single women teachers . . . The Court held that it was valid, see *SHORT -v-POOLE CORPORATION* Warrington L.J. (1926) ch. 66 stated the familiar circumstances in which a policy might be held Ultra vires 'It may be possible to show that an act . . . was so clearly founded on alien and irrelevant grounds as to be outside the authority conferred upon the body' . . . in short, if the policy is one which could reasonably be upheld for good educational reasons it is valid.

The Education Act 1981 is rich in subjective language and, generally speaking, it is easy to identify those sections which permit the local education authority, governors, or Secretary of State a discretion. Sections 2(2) and 2(3) of the Act are more difficult to interpret since it is not entirely clear to what extent, if any, those provisions confer a discretion upon the local education authority.

It will be recalled that where a local education authority maintain a statement in respect of a child, there is a duty if two conditions 'are satisfied', to secure that the child is educated in an ordinary school.[7] The conditions are that account has to be taken of the views of the child's parent, and that educating the child in an ordinary school is compatible with three objectives, (namely, his receiving the special provision he requires, the provision of efficient education for the children with whom he will be educated and the efficient use of resources). There are two ways in which these provisions may be considered. On one view, they do not allow the local education authority any discretion in deciding whether or not the conditions are satisfied. It is a strict test, which is, are the conditions satisfied? Section 2(2) provides that the duty to educate in an ordinary school arises 'if the conditions mentioned in sub-section 3 are satisfied'. There is no reference to the 'opinion' of the local education authority, or to the authority 'being satisfied that' the conditions are complied with. However, on another view, it could be argued that the whole tenor of the Act is so subjective in that it leaves wide areas of discretion open to local education authorities, that it must have been intended that local education authorities should have some discretion as to whether or not the Section 2 conditions are complied with.[8] This argument is supported by a close analysis of the objectives specified in Section 2(3). For example, the 'efficient use of resources' is a matter which it is difficult to assess objectively. It is a matter about which the authority are in the best position to exercise judgment. It could also be argued that, had Parliament intended that the question of whether or not these conditions have been complied with be judged objectively, Parliament would have specified the criteria to be applied in making such a judgment. It is submitted however, that the proper approach to Section 2(2) and Section 2(3) is to apply an objective approach to the particular local education authority in question. In other words the proper test ought to be stated in this way — considering the resources and provisions available to this particular local education authority, are these conditions satisfied? It is submitted that such an interpretation gives effect to the literal effect of the provisions. Had Parliament intended to confer a discretion upon the local education authority it would have made that quite clear as it has done elsewhere in the Act.

The Procedure for an Application for Judicial Review

There is a general principle that judicial review will only be granted when all other remedies have been exhausted so that an applicant for judicial review is unlikely to be successful if he has not first exhausted the statutory appeals procedures available to him. Until recently it was common for individuals to seek to enforce Public Law Rights by way of ordinary action in the High Court or County Court by seeking a declaration together with damages.[9] However, in *O'REILLY and OTHERS -v- MACKMAN and OTHERS* (1982) 2 WLR 1096 the House of Lords held that it was both contrary to public policy and an abuse of process of the court for a plaintiff complaining of a public authority's infringement of his public law rights to seek redress by way of ordinary action.

The procedure to be followed in an application for judicial review is contained in Order 53 of the Supreme Court Practice. The particular order sought will usually be that of mandamus, requiring the authority or individual in question to do a particular act in furtherance of a duty, power or discretion. However, since the commencement of the new Order 53 procedure, there is now no necessity upon an application for judicial review to specify the particular prerogative order required. The applicant must specify the relief claimed, this will usually involve an application for a declaration and an injunction. Damages may be claimed, but they will only be awarded where a claim for damages has been included in the statement in support of the application.

The application for judicial review is made to the Divisional Court of the High Court and must be preceded by an application for leave to apply for judicial review. The application for leave is made ex-parte to a Judge by filing form No: 86A, together with an affidavit verifying the facts relied on, at the Crown Office. If the application for leave is refused by the Judge the applicant may renew his application before a single Judge sitting in Open Court, or, if the Court so directs, to the Divisional Court of the High Court.

An application for judicial review should be made 'promptly' and in any event within 3 months from the date when grounds for the application first arose, unless the court considers that there are good grounds for extending the period. The application for judicial review is by way of originating motion to a Judge sitting in Open

Court. The notice of motion or summons must be served on all persons directly affected. The motion must be entered for hearing within 14 days after the Grant of Leave. The applicant must also serve any statement and affidavit in support of his application on all directly affected persons together with the notice of motion. The rules of the Supreme Court now include procedures for discovery, interrogatories and cross-examination. Legal aid is available to applicants for judicial review.

Commissions for Administration: the Ombudsman

Whilst the referral of a case to the local ombudsman is not, strictly speaking, an appeal, it is a further course open to a parent wishing to challenge a decision of a local education authority. The task of the local ombudsman is to investigate complaints of maladministration such as delay, bias, or incompetence. The ombudsman is not permitted to investigate complaints about the internal affairs of schools such as curriculum, internal organisation, management and discipline. Nor is the ombudsman permitted to investigate any action in respect of which the complainant has had a right of appeal to a statutory tribunal or minister. However, he is empowered to investigate complaints about most other aspects of education including complaints about the local appeals committees and about educational provision under the Act.

Complaints to the ombudsman should be made in writing through a councillor. If the councillor refuses to refer a complaint to the ombudsman there is provision for the complaint to be submitted directly. The difficulty with referring matters to the local ombudsman is that investigations tend to be lengthy and consequently, in cases where there are grounds for judicial review, an aggrieved parent who bides his time waiting for the decision of the ombudsman may find that he is out of time for an application for judicial review.

Notes

1. Except that, if the local education authority's arrangements for the admission to school provide for the admission of children who will attain the age of 5 within 6 months of admission, it applies to such children.

2. The Code of Guidance is designed to create uniformity between the various local committees, its provisions may be persuasive as to what is reasonable practice, but they are in no sense legally binding.

3. As to appeals under the Education Act 1980, see pages 76–77.

4. These general powers do not apply to non-maintained schools.

5. This includes the Education Act 1981.

6. See page 73.

7. See page 24.

8. This approach was adopted recently by the House of Lords in *R -v- HOME SECRETARY* (ex-parte ZAMIR) (1980) A.C. 930. Under the Immigration Act 1971 an Immigration Officer may detain an illegal entrant who may then be removed from the country by the Home Secretary. An 'illegal entrant' is defined in the Act as a person entering or seeking to enter unlawfully. In this case the question was whether Mr Zamir had entered this country unlawfully or lawfully. The statute involved no subjective language. However, the House of Lords held that 'the whole scheme of the Act' indicated a subjective approach. Consequently, the court could only intervene if the Home Secretary was behaving in a way that no reasonable Home Secretary should.

9. This continues to be a proper course where the desire to enforce a public law right is merely collateral to an action for damages, see *COCKS -v- THANET DISTRICT COUNCIL* (1982) 3 WLR 1121.

12 DISCLOSURE AND INSPECTION OF REPORTS AND DOCUMENTS

Significance

Obviously the parent of a statemented child is entitled to have sight of the statement; that is one of the purposes of Section 7 of the Act and of the requirement that a child's special educational needs be recorded in a statement. It can be seen from the 'proposed form' of statement[1] that the 'proposed form' has 7 appendices under the following headings, 'parental representation', 'parental evidence', 'educational advice', 'medical advice', 'psychological advice', 'other advice obtained by education authority', and 'information furnished by the district health authority or social services authority'. These appendices will include advice submitted to the local education authority under Regulation 4 of the Education (Special Educational Needs) Regulations 1983.[2] The Secretary of State has given certain advice, concerning the information to be included in the appendices of the statement in Paragraph 37 of the DES circular 1/83:

> The professional advice on which the local education authority make their decision must be copied verbatim in the appendices to the statement. Professionals should be aware that their advice will be made available to the parent, and in the event of an appeal, to the appeal committee. The professional advice should relate to the assessment of the child's special educational needs and how these should be met. There should be no need to include other details whose communication might give rise to problems of confidentiality or professional ethics.

There may be instances where specialist advisors are in possession of or submit advice to local education authorities, additional to that advice which is to be included in the appendices to the statement. This seems to be implicit in the last sentence of paragraph 37 of DES circular 1/83. In such cases the local education authority may for some reason, for example, confidentiality or professional ethics, refuse to allow the parent of the child concerned to inspect the contents of the documents or reports which contain the additional or further advice. Whilst the local education authority may feel that it is justified in withholding such reports and documents, the parent may also feel that his case is unduly prejudiced by his not having inspected them. It may be that the authority has taken something into account which it should not have done or something which the parent would have been able to rebut or elucidate in some way. In civil proceedings the rules of procedure require that each party disclose 'a list of the documents' relevant to the case that he has in his possession. There is also provision for each party to inspect all relevant documents in the possession of the other side. These procedures are designed to ensure that justice is done to all parties to the proceedings and that no party to the proceedings is prejudiced because he is unaware or has not had sight of a relevant document.

Disclosure in Proceedings for Judicial Review

Under order 53 rule 8 of the Rules of the Supreme Court the Court may grant an interlocutory order for the discovery and inspection of documents. The general approach to discovery and inspection of documents is that all relevant documents should be disclosed and that inspection of documents shall be permitted. There are, however, important exceptions to this proposition. In such cases documents are said to be 'privileged'.

Legal Professional Privilege

All direct communications between a party and his legal advisor are privileged, including communications before litigation was contemplated. Documents may also be protected by legal professional privilege if they are prepared by a third party. To be so protected the documents must have been prepared by the third party for submission to the litigant's solicitor in order to enable the solicitor to advise his client. For example, a report concerning the special educational needs of a child prepared by an educational psychologist employed by an authority would ordinarily not be privileged under this exception, since the purpose of the report is to advise the authority as to the child's needs, and is not a purpose related to prospective litigation.

However, if such a report was prepared for submission to a local education authority's solicitor in order to assist the solicitor in determining whether or not another educational psychologist had reached a valid conclusion in an advice which had been included in a statement which was the subject of legal proceedings, that subsequent report, it is submitted, would be protected by legal professional privilege.

The test as to whether or not a legal professional privilege arises in relation to documents prepared by a third party was stated by the House of Lords in *WAUGH -v- BRITISH RAILWAYS BOARD* (1979) WLR(H.L.) 150. The Plaintiff's husband was employed by the defendants. He died as a result of injuries sustained in a train collision. It was the defendants' practice to prepare three different reports, one of which was the joint enquiry report which incorporated statements of witnesses to the accident and which was sent to an inspectorate for the Department of the Environment. The heading of the report stated that it was finally to be sent to the board's solicitor for the purpose of enabling him to advise the board. The defendants refused to disclose this report and argued that it was sufficient that one of the principal purposes for which the report was prepared was for submission to the board's solicitor to enable him to advise upon liability. The House of Lords rejected this argument and reversed the decision of the Court of Appeal which had been in line with the earlier authorities of *OGDEN -v-LONDON ELECTRIC RAIL & CO.* (1973) L.T. 476 and *BIRMINGHAM & MIDLAND MOTOR OMNIBUS CO. -v-LONDON AND NORTH WINTERS RAILWAY* (1913) L.T. 109. These cases decided that legal professional privilege would be claimed where the submission of a document to legal advisors was one of the purposes for which the document was intended. In overruling these decisions Lord Wilberforce said:

> On principle I would think that the purpose of preparing for litigation ought to be either the sole purpose or at least the dominant purpose of it, to carry the protection further into cases where that purpose was secondary with another purpose would

seem to be excessive and unnecessary in the interests of encouraging truthful revelation.

It is now clear therefore that in relation to documents prepared by a third party, legal professional privilege will only be available where the purpose of preparing for litigation is the sole or dominant purpose for which the report was prepared.

Public Interest

There may be instances where it can be said to be in the public interest that documents are not disclosed. The approach adopted by the courts in such instances is by no means clear. It is however possible to discern two general approaches. These approaches may be loosely determined the 'broad approach' and the 'narrow approach'. The 'broad approach' advocates a 'balancing opera- tion' involving conflicting public interests. On the one hand there is the public interest in ensuring that all relevant evidence is disclosed, and on the other hand there is the public interest of safeguarding some important public interest. The 'narrow approach' advocates that there are certain clearly defined classes of case where a privilege may arise on the grounds of public interest. These 'classes' include those cases where 'affairs of state' are involved (for example, the interest of national security) and those cases which have been loosely termed the 'informer cases'. This latter class of case has evolved from the police informer cases where it was argued that the interests of crime detection required that police informer sources be protected.

Both approaches were ventilated in the House of Lords in *D. -v-NATIONAL SOCIETY FOR THE PREVENTION OF CRUELTY TO CHILDREN (NSPCC)* (1978) A.C. 171(H.L.). In this case the Plaintiff's health had suffered after an inspector employed by the NSPCC appeared at her house and told her that information had been received that she was maltreating her child. This suggestion was untrue, and had been made as a result of information received by the NSPCC from a member of the public.

It was the practice of the NSPCC to obtain information and assistance from the general public by promising secrecy to informants. The Plaintiff in this case sought information regarding the complaint made to the NSPCC, and it was claimed by the NSPCC that the information was privileged. The arguments put forward on their behalf were twofold: first, an argument based on confidentiality, and second, that to hold otherwise would deter informants. The House of Lords unanimously rejected the first argument and accepted the second. However, certain dicta of the Law Lords have given rise to some confusion. Lord Edmund Davies implied that he favoured a broad approach based upon a 'balancing operation' between conflicting public interests. On the one hand, that of ensuring that all relevant evidence is disclosed, and on the other hand, that of safeguarding the anonymity of the informant. Lord Hailsham of St Marylebone favoured a similar approach, for in dismissing the argument based upon confidentiality as a basis of 'immunity', he said:

There are however cases when confidentiality is itself a public interest and one of these is where information is given to an authority charged with the enforcement and administration of the law by the initiation of court proceedings. This is one of those cases, whether the recipient of the information be the police, the local authority or the N.S.P.C.C. Whether there be other cases, and what these may be, must fall to be decided in the future. The categories of public interest are not closed and must alter from time to time whether by restriction or extension, as social conditions and social legislation develop.

The dicta of Lord Edmund Davies and Lord Hailsham have been disapproved by Lord Scarman in *SCIENCE RESEARCH COUNCIL -v- NASSE* (1980) A.C.1028. Whilst in this case the House of Lords were primarily concerned with the rules for discovery of documents in Industrial Tribunal and Race Discrimination cases the law relating to privilege founded on the public interest was reviewed by the House of Lords. Lord Scarman referred to the 'very special case of *D. -v- NSPCC*'. He went on to say:

But I would with respect, not go as far as my noble and learned friend Lord Hailsham when he said in that case 'the categories of public interest are not closed'; nor can I agree with the dictum of my noble and learned friend, Lord Edmund Davies at P245 that, where a confidential relationship exists and disclosures would be in breach of some ethical or social value including the public interest, the court may uphold a refusal to disclose relevant evidence, if, on balance, the public interest would be better served by excluding it.

I do not find anything in *CONWAY -v- RIMMER* or the cases therein cited which would extend public interest immunity in this way. On the contrary, the theme of Lord Reed's speech is that the immunity arises only if 'disclosure would involve a danger of real prejudice to the national interest'. The Public interest protected by the immunity is that 'harm shall not be done to the nation or the public service by disclosure'. Whatever may be true generally of the categories of public interest, the public interest immunity, which prevents documents from being produced or evidence from being given, is restricted and is not, in my judgment, to be extended either by demanding Ministers or by the courts. And, although I agree with my noble and learned friend Lord Edmund Davies in believing that a court may refuse to order production of a confidential document if it takes the view that justice does not require its production, I do not see the process of decision as a balancing act. If the document is necessary for fairly disposing of the case, it must be produced, notwithstanding its confidentiality. Only if the document should be protected by public interest immunity, will there be a balancing act. And then that balance will not be between 'ethical or social' values of a confidential relationship involving the public interest and the documents relevant in the litigation, but between the public interest represented by the State and its public service, i.e. the executive government, and the public interest in the administration of justice: see per Lord Reed (1968) 1 AER 874 at 880 (1968) A.C. 910 at 940. Thus my emphasis would be different from that of my noble and learned friends. 'Public interest immunity' is, in my judgment restricted to what must be kept secret for the protection of Government at the highest level and in the truly sensitive areas of executive responsibility.

Lord Frazer in *SCIENCE RESEARCH COUNCIL -v- NASSE* referred to the dicta of Lord Hailsham in *D. -v- NSPCC* where Lord Hailsham had said that the categories of public interest were not closed. However, Lord Frazer argued that if that were the case, the new categories would have to be analogous to those already existing.

Despite the strong views expressed by Lord Scarman and Lord Frazer in *SCIENCE RESEARCH COUNCIL -v- NASSE*, since *D. -v- NSPCC*, the lower courts, including the Court of Appeal, have tended to adopt the balancing approach. In *GASKIN -v- LIVER-POOL COUNCIL (C.A.)* (1981) WLR 1549, Lord Denning M.R. said:

> As always in these cases, it is a matter of balancing the public interest. The Judge did not balance them in accordance with the tests which have been laid down in the authorities . . . I am left in no doubt that it is necessary for the proper functioning of the Child Care Service that the confidentiality of the relevant documents should be preserved. This is a very important service to which the interest — also very important — of the individual must, in my judgement bow. I have no doubt that the public interest will be better served by refusing discovery, and this I do.

GASKIN -v- LIVERPOOL COUNCIL was a case where a Plaintiff, who was 21 years old, had been in care until he was 18. He claimed to be suffering from severe psychological injuries which he attributed to the negligence and/or breach of statutory duty of the Liverpool City Council whilst he was in care. Clearly, discovery and inspection of the records kept upon him whilst he was in care were of the utmost importance, the Court Appeal nevertheless ruled that the records were privileged.

In considering the likely approach of the courts when considering questions of public interest privilege arising in cases under the Education Act 1981 it is important to bear in mind the underlying philosophy of the Act which emphasises throughout the role of the parent. Paragraph 6 of the DES circular 1/83 states:

> In looking at the child as a whole person, the involvement of the child's parent is essential. Assessment should be seen as a partnership between teachers, other professionals and parents, in a joint endeavour to discover and understand the nature of the difficulties and needs of individual children. Close relations should be established and maintained with parents and can only be helped by frankness and openness on all sides.

With these considerations in mind it is possible to posit the following:

(i) It is now beyond doubt that confidentiality is not a ground for the non-disclosure of a report.

(ii) If one applies the narrow approach to public policy privilege it is unlikely that cases arising under the Education Act 1981 will fall within the existing 'classes' of privilege.

(iii) Whilst it is questionable whether the broad approach can withstand a close scrutiny of the authorities, it is clear that it has found favour with the courts. However, applying the broader approach, the interests of the child concerned will usually be decisive. Further it is submitted that a significant consideration in such a balancing operation should be the public interest in ensuring that the underlying philosophy of the Act be preserved, namely that the parents of children with special educational needs be closely involved in making decisions affecting the education of their children. It is inconceivable that a parent could play a proper and effective part in the decision making process if he is not to be appraised of all relevant facts; that of course is why Parliament has provided that parents should be served with copies of statements including the relevant 'advices' so that they are aware of matters which have affected the decisions of the authority.

(iv) Where the interest of the child concerned require that a particular document is not disclosed the court will refuse such disclosure as part of its inherent jurisdiction in relation to children. This approach was expressed by Lord Simon of Glaisedale in *D. -v- NSPCC*: 'the first question . . . is not so much to canvass general principle as to ascertain whether the law has recognised an existing head of public policy which is relevant to the case. Of that there can be no doubt. The need for continuity in society, the legal application to children of the traditional roll of the Crown as parens patriae; its exercise in the Court of Chancery in such a way as to make the welfare of a child the first and paramount consideration in matters of custody and guardianship . . . all this tests beyond question a public interest in the protection of children from neglect or ill-usage.

In Appeals to Local Appeals Committees

What are a parent's right to inspect documents which a local education authority refuses to produce in an appeal to a local appeals committee? The Act does not contain any provisions (other than the provisions relating to the preparation and service of statements contained in Section 7 of the Act) for the discovery or production of documents in appeals to the local appeals committees. A code of practice for appeals to the local appeals committees under the Education Act 1980 was drawn up by the Association of Metropolitan Authorities in consultation with the Council on Tribunals. An addendum to this code, which relates specifically to the Education Act 1981, has been issued, and extracts from the code and the addendum are included in the appendices to this book. Neither the code nor the addendum make specific reference to discovery and inspection of documents in appeal proceedings to local appeal committees save to reserve all matters of procedure to the discretion of the committees.

The only means by which it would be open to an appellant to challenge a ruling of the committee that a document was privileged would be by way of judicial review.[3] However, courts are reluctant to interfere with a decision of a trubunal on a procedural matter which has been made in the exercise of a discretion.[4]

Limitations on Disclosure to Third Parties

The Education (Special Educational Needs) Regulations 1983 impose restrictions on the disclosure of statements. Paragraph 11(1) provides that:

(1) Subject to the provisions of the Act of 1981 and of these Regulations, a statement in respect of a child shall not be disclosed without the parent's consent except —
(a) to persons to whom, in the opinion of the education authority concerned, the statement should be disclosed in the educational interests of the child;
(b) for the purposes of any appeal under Section 8 of the Act of 1981;
(c) for the purposes of educational research which, in the

opinion of the education authority concerned, may advance the education of children with special educational needs, if, but only if, the person engaged in that research undertakes not to publish anything contained in, or derived from, a statement otherwise than in a form which does not identify any individual concerned including, in particular, the child concerned and his parent;

(d) on the order of any court or for the purposes of any criminal proceedings, or

(e) for the purposes of any investigations under Part III of the Local Government Act 1974(a) (investigation of maladministration).

Notes

1. See Appendix 2.
2. See page 41ff.
3. See Chapter 11 as to the grounds upon which a judicial review is available.
4. A parent may also refer a grievance relating to a procedural matter to the Council on Tribunals.

APPENDIX 1: HOW TO CHALLENGE A PROPOSED STATEMENT — FLOW CHART (S7 EDUCATION ACT 1981)

After service of statement
upon parent

(within 15 days beginning on the date when the Statement was served or, if Section 7(5) meetings have been arranged, within 15 days of the date fixed for the first of these meetings)

(within 15 days of service of proposed statement)

Make Representations
(Section 7(4)(a))

Request a Meeting
(Section 7(4)(b))

If parent agrees: no further action

If parent disagrees: he may follow Section 7(4)(b) procedure

If parent agrees: no further action

If parent disagrees: he may require a further meeting (Section 7(5)) within 15 days of date fixed for first meeting, or make Section 7(4)(a) representations

APPENDIX 2: 'PRESCRIBED FORM' OF STATEMENT OF SPECIAL EDUCATIONAL NEEDS

1 – INTRODUCTION

1. In accordance with Section 7 of the Education Act 1981 and the Education (Special Educational Needs) Regulations 1982 the following statement is made by the .... Council ('the education authority') in respect of the child whose name and other particulars are mentioned below.

CHILD

Surname ....   Other Names ....

Home Address ....

Date of Birth ....   Sex ....

Religion ....

Home Language ....

CHILD'S PARENT OR GUARDIAN

Surname ....   Other Names ....

Home Address ....   Relationship to child ....

2. When assessing the child's special educational needs the authority took into consideration, in accordance with Regulation 8 of the Regulations the representations, evidence and advice set out in the Appendices to this statement.

116

(ii) SPECIAL EDUCATIONAL NEEDS

(Here, set out, in accordance with Section 7 of the 1981 Act, the child's special educational needs as assessed by the education authority.)

(iii) SPECIAL EDUCATIONAL PROVISION

(Here specify, in accordance with Regulation 10(1)(a), the special educational provision which the education authority consider appropriate to meet the needs specified in Part (ii).)

(iv) APPROPRIATE SCHOOL OR OTHER ARRANGEMENTS

(Here specify, in accordance with Regulation 10(1)(b), the type of school and any particular school which the education authority consider appropriate for the child or the provision for his education otherwise than at a school which they consider appropriate.)

(v) ADDITIONAL NON-EDUCATIONAL PROVISION

(Here specify, in accordance with Regulation 10(1)(c) any such additional provision as is there mentioned or record that there is no such additional provision.)

(Signature of Authenticating Officer)

(Date)   (A duly authorised Officer of the
                                    Education Authority)

Appendix A

PARENTAL REPRESENTATIONS

(Here set out any written representations made by the parent of the child in pursuance of Section 5(3)(d) of the Act and a summary which the parent has accepted as accurate of any representations so made or record that no such representations were made.)

Appendix B

PARENTAL ADVICE

(Here set out any written evidence either submitted by the parent of the child in pursuance of Section 5(3)(d) of the Act or submitted at his request or record that no such evidence was submitted.)

Appendix C

EDUCATIONAL ADVICE

(Here set out the advice obtained in pursuance of Regulation 4(1)(a).)

Appendix D

MEDICAL ADVICE

(Here set out the advice obtained in pursuance of Regulation 4(1)(b).)

Appendix E

PSYCHOLOGICAL ADVICE

(Here set out the advice obtained in pursuance of Regulation 4(1)(c).)

Appendix F

OTHER ADVICE OBTAINED BY EDUCATION AUTHORITY

(Here set out any advice obtained in pursuance of Regulation 4(1)(d) or record that no such advice was sought.)

Appendix G

INFORMATION FURNISHED BY DISTRICT HEALTH AUTHORITY OR SOCIAL SERVICES AUTHORITY

(Here set out any such information as is maintained in Regulation 8(d) or record that no such information was furnished.)

APPENDIX 3: DES CIRCULAR 1/83 — ADVICE ON SPECIAL EDUCATIONAL NEEDS: SUGGESTED CHECK LIST

See page 55 as to the use of this check list.

Description of the Child's Functioning

1. Description of the child's strengths and weaknesses
    Physical state and functioning
    (Physical health, developmental function, mobility, hearing, vision)
    Emotional state
    (Link between stress, emotions and physical state)
    Cognitive functioning
    Communication skills
    (Verbal comprehension, expressive language, speech)
    Perceptual and motor skills
    Adaptive skills
    Social skills and interaction
    Approaches and attitudes to learning
    Educational attainments
    Self image and interests
    Behaviour

2. Factors in child's environment which lessen or contribute to his needs
    In the home and family
    At school
    Elsewhere

3. Relevant aspect of the child's history
    Personal
    Medical
    Educational

120

Aims of Provision

1. General areas of development
   Physical development
   (e.g. to develop self-care skills)
   Motor development
   (e.g. to improve co-ordination of hand and fingers, to achieve hand-eye co-ordination)
   Cognitive development
   (e.g. to develop the ability to classify)
   Language development
   (e.g. to improve expressive language skills)
   Social development
   (e.g. to stimulate social contact with peers)

2. Any specific areas of weakness or gaps in skills acquisition which impede the child's progress
   (e.g. short-term memory deficits)

3. Suggested methods and approaches
   Implications of the child's medical condition
   (e.g. advice on the side-effects of medication for epilepsy)
   Teaching and learning approaches
   (e.g. teaching methods for the blind or deaf, or teaching through other specialised methods)
   Emotional climate and Social Regime
   (e.g. type of regime, size of class or school, need for individual attention)

Facilities and Resources

1. Social equipment
   (e.g. physical aids, auditory aids, visual aids)

2. Specialist facilities
   (e.g. for incontinence, for medical examination treatment and drug administration)

3. Special educational resources
   (e.g. specialist equipment for teaching children with physical or sensory disabilities, non-teaching aids)

4. Other specialist resources
    (e.g. nursing, social work, speech therapy, occupational therapy, physiotherapy, psychotherapy, audiology, orthoptics)

5. Physical environment
    (e.g. access and facilities for non-ambulant pupils, attention to lighting environment, attention to acoustic environment, attention to thermal environment, health-care accommodation)

6. School organisation and attendance
    (e.g. day attendance, weekly boarding, termly boarding, relief hostel accommodation)

7. Transport

APPENDIX 4: EXTRACTS FROM THE CODE OF PRACTICE ON APPEALS TO LOCAL COMMITTEES
(incorporating extracts from the addendum)

1. The authority should establish a panel of persons from whom appeals committees can be constituted, including parents wherever possible . . . and authorities should have regard to the desirability of including (on each Committee) a parent or parents whenever possible.

    The statutory provisions governing the membership of appeal committees considering appeals under the 1981 Act are the same as for committees considering appeals under the 1980 Act. However, the Department of Education and Science has expressed the view that an appeal committee dealing with an appeal under the 1981 Act should contain at least one person with some knowledge of special education, and the local education authority will no doubt wish to include a person with this expertise whenever possible.

2. An authority should establish by resolution the procedure for selection of the membership of panels and thereafter of appeal committees and for the appointment on each occasion of a chairman. (Paragraphs 2, 3 and 4 of the Code of Practice are not relevant to the Education Act 1981 Appeals.)

3. *Absence of member of Appeal Committees*
    Because the Act requires that a certain proportion be maintained as between the qualifications for membership of appeals committees and that they consist of three, five or seven persons, the absence of a member during the proceedings and when a decision is reached may invalidate the proceedings. If a member is unable to remain, then the appeal committee, if of sufficient size, may be re-constituted as a smaller number within the statutory provisions, but if proceedings have commenced the consent of the parties should be obtained to such re-constitution. Failing that, the appeal must be re-heard

123

before a fresh committee, the 14 day notice requirement not applying provided that reasonable arrangements are agreed with the appellant.

4. *Clerk to the Committee*

Each appeal committee should have the services of a clerk. If the committee withdraws or invites the parties to do so, when it wishes to consider its decision, the clerk may remain with the committee on the invitation of the chairman but only for the purpose of offering advice as to procedure or the law.

The clerk may be the Chief Executive, secretary or appropriate officer of the local education authority, and he will be responsible for supplying the necessary staff, for allocating appeals to appeals committees and for ordering the business . . . the person attending an appeal committee as clerk to that committee should not be an employee who in the course of his employment by the authority or the schools, or schools concerned, deals with the admission of children to schools.

5. *Procedures before Notice of Appeal*

. . . the Department of Education and Science has expressed the hope that the appeal procedure will be used as little as possible, and clearly local education authorities will wish to accommodate the wishes of parents wherever possible. The continuation of established good practices in this respect by way of a 'non-statutory' extension to the discussions envisaged by the Act would, therefore, be desirable, though clearly each local education authority would have to fix a reasonable limit in each case beyond which they feel further discussion would be fruitless. The procedure for the preparation of a formal statement under Section 7 of the Education Act 1981 amounts to a statutory consultation process with the parent by the service of a copy of the proposed statement on the parent, and the right of the parent to make representations to the local education authority about the content of the proposed statement, to require a meeting with an officer of the Authority, and then to require a subsequent meeting or meetings, if necessary. Section 7(7) of the Education Act 1981 specifies a time limit of 15 days within which each of these parental rights may be exercised.

6. *Notice of Appeal*
An appeal under the 1981 Act must be in writing setting out the grounds on which it is made, and the local education authority should consider devising a pro-forma including guidance for parents which should be given to those parents who express dissatisfaction with the formal statement in accordance with Section 7 of the Education Act 1981.

It should be remembered that the requirement of Section 7(3)(b) of the Education Act 1981 covering the duty of a local education authority to give a written explanation of the parents rights under Section 7(4) to Section 7(7) does not relate to a parents right of appeal under Section 8 of the 1981 Act. This pro-forma should therefore give additional, clear guidance to parents on the 'next stage' in the proceedings and should set out clearly their rights in respect of an appeal and should encourage them to attend any hearing if they wish to do so. In addition . . . they should fix a time limit of not less than 14 days for parents to lodge an appeal after they have received the local education authority's formal statement.

7. *Conduct of Proceedings*
The conduct of proceedings is in the discretion of the committee and it may be appropriate to arrange the proceedings in the following order, though the committee will no doubt consider whether it would be helpful to vary this order:

(i)   Case for the appellant;
(ii)   Questioning by the authority;
(iii) The case for the authority;
(iv)   Questioning by the appellant;
(v)   Summing up by the authority;
(vi)   Summing up by the appellant.

The committee may adjourn any case to enable an appellant to attend to receive further significant evidence, because of the illness or absence of a member of the committee, or for any other appropriate reason. It should not normally be necessary for a child or other witness to attend, although the committee may consider it appropriate to allow witnesses, who have attended to give evidence, provided it is relevant and not repetitive (but see below).

8. The Department of Education and Science has expressed the wish that the appeals procedure under the Education Act 1981 should be as close as possible to that used under the 1980 Act and the procedure used in the hearing should, therefore, be that set out above. However, local education authorities should consider the following points of particular concern and relevance to Appeals under the Education Act 1981:

(a) The person conducting the appeals on behalf of the local education authority will very often be different from the person who conducts appeals under the 1980 Act and it will be important to ensure that he or she is fully familiar with the relevant procedures etc. Furthermore, the nature of the cases under the 1981 Act will often mean that witnesses are called much more often than under the 1980 Act appeals; this will apply equally to parents who may wish to call their own experts to challenge professional judgments which have been given and so the guidance (given above) should be adopted accordingly.

(b) Because there is an increased likelihood of parents seeking their own expert evidence in connection with these appeals, local education authorities should point out to them at some stage prior to the hearing that appeal committees will wish to come to a fair decision based upon a full understanding of all the evidence before them and this will be greatly assisted if parents provide copies of medical reports etc. to the Clerk of the appeal committee in good time before the hearing. The clerk will then be able to circulate such written documentation to members before a hearing and so the risk of time-consuming adjournments will be minimised.

(c) Because of the nature of some of the appeals under the Education Act 1981 and of the assessment made by various professionals in connection with the preparation of a formal statement, the need for rigorous control over, for example, the production and dissemination of copies of documents associated with appeals will be essential in order to maintain the confidentiality which is essential with appeal cases.

9. *Hearings*

On all cases a time and place of hearings should be appointed. Parents can however be advised:

(i) That they may elect not to attend, and instead allow the appeal to be considered on the written statements;

(ii) that the appeal will be decided on the information available, if having failed to give reasonable explanation, they do not appear.

Unless the appellant consents in writing to a lesser period, he should be given at least 14 days (from the date of posting) written notice of the meeting of the committee at which the appeal is to be heard. Hearings should be in premises reasonably accessible to the parents concerned; and, while consideration should be given to convening hearings at times of day convenient to parents, the volume of appeals and local circumstances may prevent such flexibility. When arranging appeal hearings, the authorities should have regard to the incidence of holiday arrangements. ... and an appeal committee should normally allow the appellant to be accompanied by a friend or to be represented unless there are good reasons to the contrary which should be given to the appellant. However, legal representation will seldom be necessary or appropriate.

The matters to be taken into account by an appeal committee in considering an appeal shall include any representations made by the appellant under Section 7 of the Education Act 1981, and since it is a statement of the local education authority's proposed special educational provision which is the subject of the appeal, the authority will wish to ensure that copies of that statement are provided for the parents, if they do not still have copies, and for the appeal committee. Parents and appeal committee members will of course be entitled to be given copies of any reports which it is intended to present to the committee.

It would be desirable, . . . whenever possible for unanimous decisions to be reached.

The appeal committee may confirm the special educational provision specified in the statement or remit the case to the local education authority for re-consideration in the light of their observations. Any observations the committee wishes to make should therefore be clear, and in writing. Parents should be informed of the appeal committee's decision in every case. It should be noted that unlike an appeal under the 1980 Act any decision made by an appeal committee does not bind the local education authority. It may be appropriate to point this fact out to the parents where a local education authority proposes to take action which does not accord with the recommendation of the appeal committee.

Parents who are dissatisfied with the decision of an appeal committee, or of a local education authority after it has been requested to reconsider a case following its remission by an appeal committee, may appeal to the Secretary of State. Parents should be informed of this further right of appeal and of the address to which they should write at the same time as they are informed of the decision of the appeal committee or the local education authority.

10. *Record of the Proceedings of an Appeal Committee*
The clerk of an appeal committee should keep brief notes of the proceedings, the attendance, the voting and the decisions in such form as the authority may agree is appropriate. Such documents will not be public.

11. *Service of Documents*
Documents required to be served under this code may be sent by post or delivered to a parent addressed to him at the address given by him to the authority.

APPENDIX 5: SPECIAL PROVISION RELATING TO ACCESS TO SCHOOL BUILDINGS

Section 8 of the Chronically Sick and Disabled Person's Act 1970 provides:

> Any person undertaking the provision of a building intended for purposes mentioned in subsection (2) below shall, in the means of access both to and within the building, and in the parking facilities and sanitary conveniences to be available (if any), make provision, in so far as it is in the circumstances both practicable and reasonable, for the needs of persons using the building who are disabled.

The Section applies to all schools within the meaning of the Education Act 1944, and to other institutions providing further education pursuant to a scheme under Section 42 of the Education Act 1944. The Section also applies to all universities and colleges.

A 'building' was defined by Byles J. in *STEVENS -v-GOURLEY* (1859) 7 CB (NS) 19 at p. 112 as 'a structure of considerable size and intended to be permanent or at least to ensure for a considerable time'. It was said in *CHESHIRE COUNTY COUNCIL -v-WOODWARD* (1962) a AER 517 that a 'building' must be a structure which forms part of the realty and change the physical character of the land. It is submitted that the question of whether or not a structure is a 'building' within the meaning of Section 8 is a question of fact to be determined in each case.

INDEX